In

"What an incredib..e book. ı ... .ne very ....M. ... .lants a seed of love and hope in your mind. With the coaching and insider's perspective that comes with the book, ideas will flourish and you will gain the confidence that you can bring the sunshine—so needed for growth—to a child's life. A must-read for those who believe in dreams as this book is proof that heaven is in the journey, not the destination.[It should be a] required read for college students, and parents! Then we would have enough mentors for all children. I talked and coached my friend Kevin through becoming a mentor, and I sure wish that I just had this book so I could of handed it to him and had him read it! I'm not sure how ANYONE could read this book and not want to become a mentor."

–KELLI PATTERSON, Teacher/Counselor Aid for At-Risk Youth,
Pressley Ridge, Parkersburg, WV

"As an educator and inspirer for thirty-four years, I found *MENTOR ME!* to be relevant, accurate, helpful and inspiring. I believe Dirkes got it right and this book is a must-read for all mentors and teachers."

–CATHY KEELER, Life Management Teacher, Hazel Park High School, Hazel Park, MI

"This is the best practical book I have read on mentoring. To the potential mentor, it offers a less intimidating process and replaces it with that of an exciting exploration. Further, this is a great tool for organizations looking to start a basic mentoring program. *MENTOR ME!* offers a solid framework mixed with key national standards and best practices. This will help potential mentors make a sound decision."

–ANNETTE KELLY, CEO/Founder, Youth Development Consultant/Trainer, For Our
Ultimate Success (FOUS) Youth Development Services, Chicago, IL

"This is a powerful book for anyone who has ever considered mentoring a child or is brand new to the opportunity. *MENTOR ME!* addresses every concern you may have about mentoring so you can be successful—fitting it into a busy schedule, how to relate to girls, how to choose activities together, how to deal with almost any issue that may arise and many others. The comments and poems by Chelsea are wonderful. The stories about Paula and Chelsea make it very real and show the reader specifically how to handle issues that arise. I want to use this book in my Mentor Training sessions! The 'Conversation Starters' are excellent as well as the questions about boundaries [that should be observed]—GREAT!"

–DARLENE L. RUSSELL, Site Coordinator for Mentoring Children of Promise Program,
Volunteers of America of Western New York

"MENTOR ME! is interactive, informative and genuine. As a long-time mentor, I know the nervous anticipation aspiring mentors face. Paula helps guide you through the process with real-life examples, humorous prose and insightful resources. After reading this guide, your path will be clear. "

–RASHEDA KAMARIA, CEO, Empowered Flower Girl LLC, Detroit, MI

"An inspirational book for anyone interested in mentoring. This book answered my questions and provided insight into what mentoring is really like. Although it is written from a woman's perspective, the information is very applicable to men and mentoring."

– CHARLES HAILEY, Future Mentor, Troy, MI

"You had me at Chapter 1! After years of watching my friends mentor girls, I finally understand what mentoring actually is as well as how much I can offer to, and gain from, a mentoring relationship. Sign me up! Paula takes all the guesswork out of how to be a mentor and what to do next!"

–LANDI HELLER, Future Mentor, Royal Oak, MI

"Paula has written a compelling argument for mentoring and defined the standard by which any reasonably sane woman can decide to become a mentor. Paula—and her star mentee, Chelsea—are an inspiration and reminder that we CAN make room in our hearts and diaries for this humbling role."

–LORRAINE HIRST, Resilience Coach and Mentoring Programme Developer,
Way2Be.me, Northampton, U.K.

"Paula Dirkes has provided an essential guidebook for any women questioning whether they should mentor. By the end of the book you'll be convinced that mentoring is for you!"

–KATIE HOLDEN, Director, Mentor Connection,
Jewish Family Service, West Bloomfield, MI

"MENTOR ME! is a fantastic book—an intelligently written, comprehensive guide to mentoring girls that is both highly practical and deeply inspirational. I loved how it reveals the life-changing power of mentoring from both the mentor's and mentee's perspective. I eagerly look forward to sharing it with others!"

–SERGIO BARONI, Psychotherapist, Life Coach,
Professional Mentor, Corte Madera, CA

Mentor Me!

THE COMPLETE GUIDE FOR WOMEN WHO WANT TO MENTOR GIRLS

By

PAULA C. DIRKES

With

CHELSEA M. McKINNEY

Future Generations Publishing

4t "/18 $19.95

MENTOR ME! THE COMPLETE GUIDE FOR WOMEN WHO WANT TO MENTOR GIRLS
Copyright © 2012 by Paula Dirkes

Cover design by: Heather Kirk
Interior design and typeset by: Laura Bramly

Printed in the United States of America.

ISBN-13 978-0-98379-360-1
ISBN-10 0-98379-360-3

Future Generations Publishing
29488 Woodward Ave. Ste. 446
Royal Oak, MI 48073
Contact us:
www.MentorMeBook.com
Email: info@MentorMeBook.com

Disclaimer

This book is designed to provide information on how to be a mentor to a girl. It is sold with the understanding that the publisher and author are not engaged in rendering child psychology, child-rearing, counseling or other professional services. If such advice is required, the services of a competent professional should be sought—ideally through the mentoring organization with whom you are a mentor volunteer.

It is not the purpose of this guidebook to reprint all the information that is otherwise available to youth mentors, but instead to complement, amplify and supplement other texts. You are urged to read all the available material, learn as much as possible about youth mentoring and tailor the information to your individual needs. For more information, see the many resources on this website: www.youthmentorideas.com under the various "Resources" tabs toward the top.

Every effort has been made to make this guidebook as complete and accurate as possible. However, there may be mistakes, both typographical and in content. Therefore, this text should be used only as a general guide and not as the ultimate source of youth mentoring information. Furthermore, this manual contains information on youth mentoring that is current only up to the printing date.

All website addresses, e-mail addresses and contact phone numbers provided in this book were accurate at the time of writing.

The purpose of this guidebook is to educate and (possibly) entertain. The author and Future Generations Publishing shall have neither liability nor responsibility to any person or entity with respect to any loss or damage caused, or alleged to have been caused, directly or indirectly, by the information contained in this book.

If you do not wish to be bound by the above, you may return this book to the publisher for a full refund.

To all the dedicated, busy youth mentors of the world who reprioritize their lives to be consistently available, to open up their lives and hearts, to be open-minded and nonjudgmental and to be a rich source of caring and support. You make children feel important and special and you create the magic of mentoring.

— Paula —

I would like to dedicate this book to my two most motivating teachers: Teri Cohodes and Amy Carpenter. Through the toughest times they were there to guide and motivate me.

— Chelsea —

To the world
you may be just one person,
but to one person
you may be the world.

– Brandi Snyder –

Contents

A Christmas Gift from My Mentee Chelsea

T-shirt reads:
"Paula—You are my best friend. Chelsea"

Acknowledgments

Paula's Acknowledgements

Chelsea Marie McKinney: You are my inspiration, my mentor, my "daughter," my pal, my music coach, my window into the life of a girl. You are absolutely Im-PRESS-ive and I love you!

The McKinney family—George, Kim, Josh, Jake, Sam, Sara and Grandma Doris: You accepted me, trusted me and welcomed me each week. Thank you! It is a pleasure knowing all of you.

Sergio Baroni: You were the catalyst behind this book! What you suggested (as my life coach) was to write a "little book of wisdom for girls." We've come a long way baby! *Mille grazie* for putting this "bug" in my ear.

Kim Stern: As my life coach, you were another constant source of encouragement for this project and you helped me keep my priorities straight and my nose to the grindstone. Thank you!

Ann McIndoo: Thank you for your help and book-writing system to get the original book "out of my head" and on to paper.

Jeff Strauch: You were my love, my best friend and always supportive of my time with Chelsea and of my writing this book. You left the planet way too soon. I will always love you.

Debbie Hasenau: Thank you for jumping in with both feet when the request for mentors went out at COT back in 2000. You truly were my inspiration to "get involved" rather than let the opportunity pass me by. I highly doubt this significant, life-changing chapter of my life would have happened if you hadn't led the way.

Mom and Dad: You were two of my most important mentors as I grew up and even well into my adulthood. Thank you both for your love and support in life and beyond. I hope the golf courses in Heaven always have tee times.

My siblings and their spouses—Jim (and Deb), Sue (and Todd) and Jessica: Thank you for your curiosity, your support and your encouragement. I love you all.

My nieces and nephews—Dan, Anna, Ruth, Grace, Gloria, Sarah, Tina, Bruno and Isabella: Thank you for being in my life! No matter what amount of time I get to see you, I always enjoy it. You helped me become a better mentor.

The Circle of Cool Women: Many thanks for being wonderful girlfriends and my constant source of laughter, support and encouragement. You really ARE cool—and not just because you're Friends of Paula.

Mark Van der Gaag: Thank you for creating and masterfully facilitating the Teen Peace Circle at RU. Your respect and love for those "young adults with less experience" was palpable and a turning point for how I understood and related to young people. All those Thursday nights with you and the teens were truly life-altering for me.

Michael J. Allen: Watching you inspire and transform so many teenagers through so many CD programs provided me with many skills and a comfort level that enabled me to be an even better mentor to Chelsea and other young people. I was especially thrilled to bring her to the community CD so she could meet you and experience the wonderful program. Thank you for being the loving presence that you are in the world.

Phyllis McCaffrey: Although we only met one time, I really recognized your love and dedication to Youth Assistance and the Mentors Plus program in Oakland County. You planted one of the seeds for this book—thank you!

Linda Patton: You were the extra-inspirational volunteer mentor who spoke (with a broken leg and walker!) at my Mentors Plus Orientation program on a cold Saturday morning in November of 2000. Your dedication spoke to me and caused me to continue down this path. Thank you!

Garry Pullins and Candy Hlivka: Thank you for taking this newbie and guiding her through the Mentors Plus Orientation and into the life-changing experience of youth mentoring.

Dawn Wolfe: Much gratitude for being the person to recognize that a "little book of wisdom for girls" was doable, but a story about the mentoring relationship that Chelsea and I shared was far more interesting. Thank you for your early guidance and editing.

Kristina Marshall of Winning Futures!: Many thanks for your interest and support of my work and for sharing your mentoring research "hot off the press." You were a critical connection that streamlined my ability to meet with other mentoring organization representatives in the Detroit area.

Jerry Lapides: Thank you for your mentorship during grad school and beyond. You've been a listening ear, a calming influence, a source of knowledge and my "Jewish Dad" during an important time in my life.

Sharon Werner: Thank you for being one of my important mentors during grad school and beyond. You are a friend, an exceptionally creative consultant and educator, and I am pleased to know you.

Mentoring enthusiasts I have met in person or by phone along the way who really "get it" about the importance of mentoring: Thanks to David Neil of Telementor.org and Christine Steele, fellow mentor and author.

AM2 Money Mind members—Mark, Willette and Russ: Thank you for your weekly encouragement, interest and patience while I learned about online marketing and becoming an author too.

Julia Gordon Applegate: Thank you for your willingness to photograph Curley the Pig for his debut in this book! Although Curley wasn't the typical "wildlife" you are used to, thank you for making an exception. (For amazing wildlife and nature photography contact Julia at: julia@ applegateimages.com.

Mary Lewis: Thank you for your listening ear during our walks and your excellent research ability. Your help is appreciated.

Veronica Jones: Thank you for your research assistance for the book as well as sharing yourself and your daughters, Delaney and Erika with Chelsea and I over the years.

Laura Bramly: Thank for your excellent book editing for this second edition. I know for certain I would never have done it unless you had been available.

To all the people I forgot to mention and should have, please forgive me and know that you made a contribution to this book as well! Thank you!

Chelsea's Acknowledgments

I want to acknowledge my family. Thank you for supporting me. For my Mom (Kimberly McKinney) and Dad, thank you for supporting me and pushing me along the way. Also, thanks to my lifelong idol and role model Paula Dirkes. Thank you all for all you do.

Preface

I was fortunate to grow up in an environment where positive role models were available to me. Early in life I learned the value of having a mentor at home, in school and even in my neighborhood.

I have been working with young people since my days at Michigan State University as a Physical Education major and student teacher. For several summers, I worked as a Park Playleader at two different community parks in my hometown of Grand Rapids, organizing activities and crafts for neighborhood kids. After graduating from MSU, I was a substitute teacher at a junior high school in Lansing, Michigan and also (ironically) served as the Cheerleading Coach for the Junior Varsity and Varsity squads at the same junior high school; I've never been a cheerleader in my life! I then worked as the Youth and Aquatic Director at the Lansing Central YMCA and was the adult advisor to the YMCA Leaders Club program for twelve- to eighteen-year-old students who volunteered in YMCA classes and events.

I took a fifteen-year break from working with youth (with the exception of being an aunt to my nieces and nephews), but returned about ten years ago to youth mentoring where I met Chelsea. I expanded my mentoring role to include working with twelve- to eighteen-year-old students in a faith-based setting and have been a repeat volunteer at local Challenge Day programs at middle and high schools. In 2008 I got involved as an adult "coach" in the Teen Leadership class at a local high school and more recently I acted as a tutor/mentor at a charter school in East Detroit.

Working with young people in a mentoring capacity has dramatically changed my life and has become an important priority and commitment to me. It definitely contributes to the person I want to be in the world.

Mentor Me

Lyrics written by Chelsea McKinney and Paula Dirkes.
Sung to the tune of "Rescue Me," lyrics and music by Fontella Bass (1965),
as sung by Aretha Franklin.

Mentor me
Oh take me to the mall
Mentor me
I want to hear you call
'Coz I'm lonely and you care
You will listen—and I may share!

Come on and mentor me
Come on lady and mentor me
Come on lady and mentor me
'Coz I need you by my side
Can't you see that I'm waiting?

Mentor me
Come on and take my hand
Take our hearts, and conquer every part
'Coz I'm lonely and you know
I need you to help me grow

Chorus: Come on and mentor me
Come on lady and mentor me
Come on lady and mentor me
'Coz we're perfect, side by side
Can't you see that I'm waiting?

Mentor me
Oh take me to the mall
Mentor me
I want to hear your call
'Coz I'm lonely and you care
You will listen—and I may share!

Come on and mentor me
Come on lady, watch me lady, listen lady, hold me lady
Can't you see that I need you lady
Can't you see that I'm waiting?
Mentor me

Come on and take my hand
Come on lady and be my friend
'Coz I need you, 'coz you want to
Can't you see that I'm waiting?
Watch me lady
Listen lady
Hold me lady
Can't you see that I'm waiting?

Mentor me, mentor me…

Introduction

My mentee Chelsea and I have been together for ten years—about nine years longer than a typical mentoring match. We wouldn't have stayed together so long if we didn't enjoy each other's company and get value out of our relationship. But it took a question from someone not familiar with mentoring to make me realize why mentoring is so special to me, and why I am committed to sharing the critical importance of mentoring with you.

In February of 2008, I was one of eight hundred participants from around the world at a Peak Potentials Training "Life Directions Intensive" seminar. One exercise had us working in pairs. I had just told my partner that I was writing a book on mentoring a child and that my greater desire was to create a worldwide "Mentoring Phenomena." She pondered this and asked, "Why is mentoring so special to you?"

Her question surprised me! I had never examined where my interest and dedication to mentoring came from; I just believed in it. I enjoyed my time with my mentee Chelsea. I knew that mentoring made a positive difference in both our lives. I felt like we had developed a wonderful relationship and Chelsea often validated my feeling by telling me she appreciated having me in her life. But after thinking for a bit, I realized that my interest in mentoring stemmed from my belief in the importance of really being heard.

When I was growing up, not only was I the fourth and last Dirkes child (last in the pecking order and with the fewest baby pictures), but I was quite the tomboy. I climbed trees, raced bicycles with the boys on the other side of the block, played Matchbox cars with Johnny down the street and made tree camps. As a preteen girl, I rebelled against my mother's attempts to "girl-ify" me and her patient appeals: "Paula, please curl your hair for church." "Paula, put on a skirt for dinner." "Paula, wash your hair." And the dreaded, "Paula, please put on a dress!"

While I struggled to be my version of Paula, dear Mom had other plans for me, as did a few of my siblings, neighbors, fellow golfers and kids on the block. Even some of my schoolmates made a point of reminding me that I didn't "fit in" with the other girls my age. All I wanted was to be me. I craved to be heard and accepted for who I was and really respected as an individual.

To a large degree, being heard was missing from my childhood and I suspected it was something that was missing from the lives of many children. I subconsciously knew that, as a mentor, I could offer a child the opportunity to be heard.

Really hearing what someone has to say is fairly rare and pretty special! When I feel really heard I feel relieved. I feel lighter! I feel respected. I feel understood. Listening is about taking in what someone says and letting it percolate through you and settle into the hills and valleys of your consciousness. Listening is about respecting what someone is saying and the way she is saying it. It's about being attentive to feelings, making eye contact and letting the person speak until finished. It could involve repeating back what the other person said to make sure you heard correctly. It's about attempting to understand where the other person is coming from instead of screening what he says through your own beliefs and values, which have no place when you are focused on really hearing what someone has to say. You are the special audience with whom that person has chosen to share what is on her mind or in her heart.

As a mentor I try to be an active, supportive and nonjudgmental listener—to truly hear what Chelsea has to say whether I agree with her or not. I might ask clarifying questions so I know exactly where she's coming from, but I really try to hold my tongue so I don't disagree with, discount or interrupt her. My goal is that she gets my focused attention when we are together.

In mentoring, giving a child the gift of being heard, of being the center of your attention every week and every month is a very special, life-changing gift. You are awarded the role of loving, supportive and absolutely dependable audience. Your mentee becomes one of your greatest fans and you become a person she truly looks up to.

Just knowing that Chelsea looks up to me as a mentor has changed me personally. I find myself being more aware of "practicing what I preach" to Chelsea regarding relationships, communication and setting boundaries. I have to be credible, not just a talking head. I really strive to be someone she can count on.

About the Book

When a positive, female, adult role model is missing from a girl's life, there is a dramatic gap. A same-sex role model is someone to emulate —an experienced female "partner" and confidante and the person who really understands the world of girls, women and the other "species" of boys and men. A male role model cannot replace the unique qualities and experience that a female role model brings to a relationship no matter how hard he tries. Girls need positive female role models. But how can busy women make time to include a girl in their lives?

Having originally balked at the idea of mentoring a child, I understand the challenges that women face in making time to mentor and validated these challenges with some online surveys. The focus of this book is therefore twofold:

- To educate the reader as to the importance of mentoring, and
- To help busy women learn to make mentoring a part of their lives and to be successful mentors.

Writing the original book began as sort of a "graduate project" that Chelsea and I could work on together. It's been a wonderful experience to share with her. Most importantly, I realized that by writing this "how to" book and sharing our mentoring stories, Chelsea and I could positively influence the future of youth mentoring around the world.

Chelsea is now twenty-one years old and is about to enter a vocational training program that she hopes will lead to a long-awaited Occupational Therapy degree. Although I am the primary author, Chelsea's creative input and contributions have made the book special, genuine and real. You will see quotes from Chelsea, which provide her "mentee" perspective, in special boxes throughout the main part of the book. Her insights not only provide a balance, but they give you the opportunity to meet this special young lady.

How this Book Will Help You

We want this book to help you make the transition from a woman who has been thinking about volunteering with kids to a woman who IS volunteering with kids. Chelsea and I hope you will see the potential for fun, personal growth, love and mutual satisfaction that is available to you through a mentoring relationship. As you read our stories and personal insights, we hope you picture yourself in similar situations and imagine how you would respond to your mentee. Start thinking about what your mentee might look like, how old she is and what activities and discussions you might share with her. Chelsea and I sincerely hope that after reading this book you will acknowledge to yourself that making this type of commitment is a weekly gift to yourself, not just another appointment to keep.

A Word About the "Men" in Mentoring

I feel compelled to mention that although this book is written to inspire busy women to mentor girls, there is plenty of evidence that indicates there is a greater shortage of men mentoring boys. I cannot personally speak from the male perspective. Nonetheless I have devoted Chapter 10 to helping women approach good men to become great mentors to boys. Women can (and do!) have influence when it comes to male decision making.

What are You Doing?
By: Chelsea McKinney

I think about what you are doing
When I am at school, where are you?
When I think of your smell, so sweet,
Or my beaten down bruises,
Do you think of me?
Will you ever mean something?
Am I a part of your heart?
Or did you let me fall
Like a crisp autumn leaf
Hitting the cool earth floor
Why should I even care?
Can't I just move on?
Knowing you left me
With no return.
I know you feel guilty
Come to your senses
Who will I become?
Without your guidance,
Without your love
The part of you in my heart
That I don't even want
I don't want to hold
You are not here anymore
My bruised soul is healed
I just want to see you and hear the words hit your lips
"My little girl I love you and I am sorry."

CHAPTER ONE

Mentoring Works, But Don't Take My Word for It!

*If you wait for the perfect moment when all is safe
and assured, it may never arrive.
Mountains will not be climbed,
races won, or lasting happiness achieved.*
— *Maurice Chevalier* —

When my mentee Chelsea was a junior in high school, she and one of her girlfriends (I'll call her Cathy) met some older boys while attending a movie near her old home town. During our weekly get together, Chelsea divulged some information about what happened that evening. She said that one of the boys acted way too forward around her. She described him as a "very touchy-feely guy," and said, "He made me feel really uncomfortable." Chelsea told me he repeatedly put his arm around her and tried to tickle her and she felt really violated as a result. She decided to let him know that she didn't like it. She told him, "Please, don't touch me. Just stop."

He asked, "Why don't you like me to touch you?"

She replied very honestly, "I don't really know you. I don't want you just touching me without saying anything."

He persisted, asking, "Why not?"

Chelsea stood her ground. "I don't have to answer that. I shouldn't have to tell you why I don't want you to touch me. You should just respect that."

Unfortunately Chelsea's friend Cathy did not have the same desire to define personal boundaries. Cathy made it clear that she wanted the attention of the boy whom she had met for the first time that evening. When Chelsea and Cathy arrived at Cathy's home to spend the night, Cathy's parents were already in bed. Cathy announced to Chelsea that she should sleep on the living room couch so Cathy could sneak her new "boyfriend" into her bedroom to have some fun. Chelsea was shocked that Cathy would be so promiscuous, let alone disrespectful to her parents across the hall. She kept wondering, "What happened to this girl I grew up with? Why don't Cathy's parents do anything to stop this? Why is Cathy acting this way with a guy she just met?"

Shortly afterward, Cathy left home and moved in with the boy, who turned out to be very controlling. She soon learned she was pregnant with the first of two children with him. Cathy never finished high school and she and her children live with her own divorced father. She has had spotty employment and her children's father has been in and out of jail. To this day Chelsea shakes her head in disbelief at how surreal Cathy's life has turned out to be. I think she thanks God that she made better choices for herself on that night back in high school.

Now twenty-one years old, my mentee Chelsea is enjoying the life of a happy, unattached young woman and has gotten quite good at assessing whether a relationship is working for her or not. She has developed the confidence to speak up when she has something to say. She has told me she would like to have children some day when she has met the right man and she has her life in order. Chelsea is happily embarking on an intensive career training program away from home.

The Need for Mentoring

Chelsea could have made very different choices as a teenager—choices about who she trusted, who she turned to for support, her education, employment, relationships, sexual activity, drugs and alcohol. Her life could have turned out very differently in any one of the ten years we have been together in a formal and informal mentoring relationship. Chelsea feels strongly that having a mentor was one of things that helped point her down a good path each time she got distracted. Unfortunately, there are so many girls that don't have a mentor or any other positive adult female role model in their lives. The shocking statistics I share with you in this chapter will make the positive impact of mentoring crystal clear.

Pregnancy and Abortion

Girls have an extra set of risks to face when growing up in a society that often exploits women through advertising, music, television, movies and even pay scale. Pregnancy and abortion are two of the biggest and most frightening risks that they face and where mentors can help. According to a 2001 UNICEF study of teenage births in the top twenty-eight "rich nations," the United States has the highest teenage birth rate in the entire developed world; 52.1 out of 1,000 girls aged fifteen to nineteen give birth to a baby. This is four times higher than the European Union. Yes, according to UNICEF, this number has dropped quite a bit over the last thirty years due to better education, more career options for women, contraception and young people making different choices, but we still maintain first place!

What about the girls that choose to end a pregnancy rather than become mothers so early in life? What about the pregnant girls who fear the repercussions from their boyfriends, parents, employers or society? According to UNICEF (2001), about half a million teenagers out of the twenty-eight OECD (Organisation for Economic Co-operation and Development) nations will seek an abortion and approximately three quarters of a million will become teenage mothers.

Thirty-five years ago there was a stigma associated with teenage pregnancy, especially in my conservative Catholic high school experience where we were taught abstinence by the nuns. (Fortunately I had Mr. Platte and he made sure contraception got covered in Biology class!) Today, based on my observations, there seems to be a resigned "acceptance" of teenage sexual activity and pregnancy by society, as if it's "just the way it is" and "there's not much we can do about it." I can't speak for you, but I'm not convinced that teenagers are somehow better equipped to deal with parenting today than we were thirty-five years ago. Through my various volunteer activities at school or church I have met teenage girls who were sexually active, became pregnant and who made the choice to have an abortion. I have talked to grown women who chose to have an abortion as teenagers. No matter what your age or circumstances, an unwanted pregnancy—let alone an abortion—is a traumatic, life-altering experience, especially with little or no support system. Mentors can share good information and life experience with girls, helping them make better choices well before an unwanted pregnancy occurs.

Parental Partnerships Affect a Child's Development

The U.S. Bureau of the Census (2006) reported that one million children are affected by divorce every year. The study found that, between 1970 and 2005, the proportion of kids living with two married parents dropped from eight-five percent to sixty-eight percent. As a long-term mentor, the way I observe the higher prevalence of divorce is that mentoring programs can fill some of the void that divorce causes, but there is a lack of caring adults to make the mentoring matches possible.

When I met Chelsea, her birth parents had been divorced for about two years. According to the caseworker who spoke to me prior to my meeting Chelsea for the first time, the divorce had taken its toll on her physically, emotionally and academically. I know it affected her siblings as well, but I did not spend time with them like I did Chelsea. Chelsea and her two younger brothers and one older sister lived with their father and only saw their mom every other weekend. I rarely saw Chelsea's birth mother, but I was aware that she lived with a man for many years and eventually married him.

According to Kurdek & Fine (1993), "The well-being of children goes down as the number of marital transitions goes up." During the ten years that Chelsea and I have been together, her three siblings and I saw her dad get involved in several relationships. He had four kids and was working full time, and so was seeking a marriage partner for himself and a mother figure for his kids. After the divorce with Chelsea's birth mother when Chelsea was nine years old, her dad dated on and off. He got married when Chelsea was thirteen and then divorced a few years later. He married again when Chelsea was twenty and it seems to be a good match for everyone. Chelsea told me once that she always looked upon every woman in her father's life as a "possible mother" because she wanted so badly to have a mother in her life. Having been an attentive listener for Chelsea over the last ten years, I know that not having her birth mother in her life severely affected her self-confidence and her self-concept, and it raised her emotional neediness to a much higher level. She has made a conscious choice to call her dad's new wife "Mom," because in her eyes, this woman is worthy of the title. I'm happy Chelsea has that sense of security.

I'm sure plenty of adults considering a mentoring opportunity can relate to the effects of their own parents divorcing. I read some research by a well-known psychologist (Emery 1988) who compared children from divorced homes to children from homes affected by death. Do you know which group had more psychological problems? The kids from a home affected by divorce. Whether it was the effects of divorce, changing parental partnerships, puberty or a combination, I watched

Chelsea says...

I never allowed myself to ever open up to any woman but Paula. She's taught me to be able to open my heart and trust that not every woman is going to stab me in the back. Not every woman is going to leave. Not every woman is like Ann, my mother, the woman that gave birth to me.

Chelsea and her siblings struggle as they grew up—especially as they entered puberty. Kids need a stable, positive adult role model to turn to during the good times and the bad. Mentors fill that gaping void.

School Attendance and Graduation

Chelsea's dad expected his kids to go to school every day and Chelsea graduated on time in 2008. That isn't the case for many children. According to *Education Week* (2010), every school day 7,200 students decide they are done going to school. For some reason that only they know, they can't handle even one more day of school. In 2010, three out of ten students walked away from high school without their diplomas; their grades and/or attendance prevented them from graduating. If you consider ethnicity, the statistics are even worse: only about fifty percent of African-Americans, Hispanic/Latino and Native American students graduate on time.

When you have under-educated kids who can't get jobs, you have more poverty, more public assistance and more health problems—since they can't afford to see a doctor. It is estimated that the United States would save seventeen billion dollars (Alliance for Excellent Education 2006) in costs related to the uninsured and Medicaid if all the high school students graduated. Over the course of a lifetime, the earning potential of a young person that doesn't graduate is $260,000 less than a high school graduate (Rouse 2005).

It may take a "village" to raise a child, but it also takes a "village" or community to educate children and keep them in school. Community-based mentoring programs play a critical role in reducing the dropout rate in the schools. A study by Tierney (1995) showed that mentored kids are fifty-two percent less likely to skip a day of school, and thirty-seven percent less likely to skip a class. Mentored kids are also more confident of their performance in schoolwork. Yet another study (Jekielele 2002) showed that mentored kids are three times more likely to be attending college two years after high school graduation.

There were many, many times that Chelsea did not want to return to school due to bullying, gossiping, teachers that didn't take the time (or have the time) to meet her educational needs (she has a learning disability), or because she was feeling "stupid" or overwhelmed. As a mentor, I listened patiently, reminded her of the things she could do, supported her to ask questions, and helped her get comfortable asking for help. I applauded her grades, efforts and accomplishments along the way and proudly took pictures of her at her high school graduation.

An important school-based mentoring study (Curtis 1999) sheds some light on the "ripple effect" of mentoring—not only in school but in the child's self-confidence level. Positive attitudes about school and personal self-confidence both improved a whopping sixty-four percent amongst mentored children. This same study showed that fifty-eight percent of the mentored kids got higher grades in important classes (social sciences, languages and math) and sixty-two percent of them were more likely to trust their teachers. Beyond the improvements with teachers and grades I can tell you firsthand, when Chelsea felt good about herself and her abilities, she was a pretty happy girl.

The benefits of mentoring leak out into the mentee's home life. Sixty percent of mentored children experienced improved relationships with adults in their lives (Curtis 1999). When Chelsea was stressing about how her dad was impatient or unavailable over the years, as a mentor I would sometimes suggest that she schedule a father-daughter date or a family meeting to discuss what was on her mind. She had brought these ideas to me before, but sometimes forgot about them and I was able to remind her of her own good ideas. More often than not, these father-daughter dates and family meetings worked to resolve what was troubling her. In addition to improved adult relationships, fifty-six percent of mentored kids have improved relationships with other children and fifty-five percent could express how they were feeling on any given day (Curtis 1999). Another study (Tierney 1995) showed that mentored kids were one-third less likely to hit someone. Trust me on this one: how the other kids were treating her and how she was feeling were huge topics throughout my mentoring relationship with Chelsea. Mentors have the power to not only reduce the high school dropout rate one hundred percent—one child at a time—but their impact touches all aspects and relationships of the child's life.

Chelsea says...

The day that I left for college, I'll never forget how proud Paula was of me, the way that she looked at me. It was a reflection on our relationship that I was actually going to college. I couldn't have done that without her ... without her encouragement, without her love and without her pushing me along the way.

Lack of Positive Adult Role Models

During summers at college, I worked at a park. I noticed little girls with faces or clothes that weren't clean. Some girls stuck to me like Velcro whenever I was at the park; they seemed to never want to go home! I wondered about it, but not for too long.

When I was student teacher during my senior year at Michigan State, there were girls in my gym classes who were confused and scared when they started their period. I wondered, "Why hasn't her mom told her all about this?" I later learned there wasn't a caring mom at home that they could turn to at this important time in their life—only a dad. It gave me pause, but I told myself, "Somebody else will step in. It's not really my job to get involved."

When I worked at the YMCA after college there were little girls who came to the monthly "Youth Overnights" whose clothes were not put on properly or whose hair hadn't been combed or shampooed in a very long time. They seemed very clingy and lacked social skills. No one at home seemed to be actively involved in their lives or their personal hygiene, nor was anyone laundering their clothes. Again, I briefly wondered about it, but I rarely saw the parents or guardian. I told myself, "It's really not my concern!"

I realized that the common element amongst these girls was the lack of positive adult role models in their lives. There are single parents that desperately care about their parenting role, but they have to work so many hours to pay the bills that they end up spending very little quality time with their children. There are other parents and guardians that had few positive role models while they grew up, so they have little understanding and skills to share with their own children. Even in wealthy families with two parents working full-time jobs, kids are often left to fend for themselves, which often means sitting in front of a computer or TV. These kids crave to be treated as importantly as a client from a parental workplace, and often act out in an attempt to get Mom or Dad's attention.

I was surfing the MENTOR/National Mentoring Partnership website the other day (www.mentoring.org) and came across a pretty shocking statistic: 17.6 million young people—nearly half the population of young people between ten and eighteen years of age—have living situations that are working against them in terms of providing support to live up to their true potential. Almost half the population! Young people are constantly trying to fit in and to be accepted. If they're not getting enough support at home, at school, at church or in their neighborhood, they may make some bad choices and suffer the consequences. I believe there are no "bad kids" at birth, but I do believe the living environment has a huge influence on the person that grows up.

Chelsea says...

I really think that any girl, and any boy, could gain something from a relationship like ours because, I mean, Paula's not another parent. Paula's a friend. She doesn't play that parental role. Teenagers always need an outward perspective on life, from an adult that has been through the same stuff, and at the same time cares about you. An outside adult is better than a parent telling you, "No, you can't do this because I'm your parent." I think everybody needs somebody to look up to and gain knowledge from that person.

The good news is that mentoring is a solution! Insert a consistent, positive adult role model into a young person's life and all of a sudden the child has a person who cares, is concerned and is a ready resource to her as she faces daily challenges. By connecting struggling children with caring adults, children are given a fighting chance to succeed! It may seem simple, but it is powerful!

Other Ways That Mentoring Helps

Plenty of research shows that growing up in poverty—due to teenage pregnancy for example—is often repeated over and over by every next generation (UNICEF 2001). Could the cycle of poverty be broken if a girl saw a different lifestyle and witnessed the choices made by her mentor? With some support and coaching, could her eyes be opened to the possibilities? I think so.

Mentors can influence the choices a child or teenager makes about nutrition, alcohol, drugs, fitness, social skills, life skills and money management—just to name a few. The Big Brothers Big Sisters organization showed proof that kids who meet regularly with their mentors are forty-six percent less likely to start using illegal drugs than kids that don't have mentors (Tierney 1995). Minority youth who met with their mentors were seventy percent less likely to start taking drugs. Where alcohol use is concerned, the kids are twenty-six percent less likely to drink when they have a stable mentoring relationship. Even more telling is that female minority youth involved in a mentoring relationship are about fifty percent less likely to drink than girls who were not mentored. Just today Chelsea was reflecting on how she now understands that she doesn't need alcohol to help her "get comfortable" socializing—that alcohol is not a solution. Making responsible choices is a solution for her.

Other positive impacts and rewards to the mentee may include:

- Having an adult friend with wisdom and who is not going to judge them
- The opportunity to run ideas past a neutral adult
- A positive, nonjudgmental adult to answer questions she might have

- Help with sorting through challenges of school, boys, peer pressure and family
- Exposure to cultural activities and shared new experiences
- Someone to provide the mentee with different options: interests, culture, practices, careers, religion
- Help with making choices or making decisions
- Increased confidence and self-esteem
- A reliable support system for her

From my own experience, support can be from one end of the spectrum to the other. Chelsea told me I was instrumental in her learning to tell time using an analog clock when she was in sixth grade. I also supported her when she had to testify in court against a relative. Never underestimate your time with a child! You never know when what you say or what you do as a mentor is going to "stick" and make all the difference in a young person's life. Recently Chelsea asked me to revisit some information I had given her four years ago about managing money. I love discovering that she was listening to me all along—being a mentor is so darn cool!

I am privileged to share with you my experience and learnings so you can be a great mentor. But being great isn't because of me; it is because you are willing to step up and listen to a child that needs you.

What Is a Youth Mentor?

A youth mentor is a caring, trustworthy adult or a "very inspirational personality" (Leenhouts 1997) willing to spend time with a child who would benefit from a positive role model who provides encouragement, assistance and some help in making good choices. A youth mentor can be anyone from a college-aged student to a retired adult. These caring adults can help a child succeed in life and make a contribution to society—especially if the child's home circumstances are not supportive.

The mentor is someone who can have an open and honest dialogue on matters that affect young people on a daily basis (bullying, peer pressure, violence and family) and has the capacity to inspire kids to be all they can be. A mentoring relationship is a very different dynamic than a parent, teacher, coach or grandparent has with a child. A youth mentor is all about support, encouragement and neutrality. A mentor has no agenda except to show up, listen and care for the child. She is not a parent, therapist, parole officer or "cool adult-sized peer."

Mentors don't have to be extra wise or a certain adult age to qualify. Over time, trust can be built and a relationship formed between a caring adult and a child who needs one. Mentoring touches and transforms both people involved in the mentoring relationship. It's an opportunity for two unrelated people from different generations to connect, learn and grow together.

Chelsea says...

My mentor is a friend, like a girlfriend, but she's not my age, so she wouldn't just say, "Oh, that boy's cute" or, "I'll do your nails for you." But she's still got that personality because she's still, like, awesome. She's like, a girl, and a friend at the same time. She's an adult and she has this love for me, and this understanding of being a human, and being a girl, 'cause she's gone through a lot of the steps of being a woman already. She also can just laugh at me because we're friends, too. I'm extremely important to Paula, and she knows how to show it to me, with the kind of love that a person needs to give somebody. She's never left me. She's never hurt me in the way that any of my family or any of my parents ever have. She's never lied to me. She shows me the love and respect that I've always wanted from a human being.

This special relationship can influence the mentee's choices involving family, friends, school, work and peer pressure. The adult has the opportunity to share her own life experience and skills with her mentee and help her sort through her day and life. In exchange, the young person can offer their own unique perspective on people and the news, the latest technology and gizmos, not to mention teaching you how to relate to people her age.

Are You Mentor Material?

> ### Chelsea says...
>
> Anyone can be a good mentor as long as you allow yourself the time and the dedication. There are so many children and girls that are just striving for love and respect for themselves.

When doing research for this book, I created a number of online surveys to assess the current-day reservations (if any) of busy women in regards to mentoring a school-aged girl. Beyond "I don't have time," the next most common theme was "I'm not sure if I have something to offer" and "I don't know how to be a mentor." I had the same insecure, doubt-filled thoughts.

Do you have what it takes to be a mentor to a girl? From my own community-based mentoring experience, I believe the two basic qualities of a mentor are: reliability and attentive listening.

If you are willing to give of your time consistently, I believe that is a great start. Adults that are reliable and dependable are often missing in your mentee's life. Once she believes you will be there for her, trust will follow. Your integrity is on the line; following through and holding yourself accountable is critical to building this relationship. She needs to know that you are going to show up and that you really care. Look upon mentoring as a way to invest in this child's life and future. You want to be the positive role model and/or the available adult that she has been missing.

Listening attentively without your own agenda is the second key quality of being a youth mentor. Do you remember when you were growing up and you started telling your mom, dad or teacher what was upsetting you? Perhaps before you even got it all out you were told, "Don't be silly! You're over-reacting! Wait until you're an adult with REAL responsibilities—then you'll know what problems are made of. Now go do your homework." Makes you feel all warm and fuzzy, doesn't it?

Chelsea says...

Some of my teachers were also my mentors—people I trusted and looked up to. One teacher was Amy Carpenter, who was there for me a good chunk of my grade school experience. When I was getting bullied at home and at school, she was someone who was there to motivate me and she also provided a shoulder to cry on. Another teacher/mentor I relied on was Teri Cohodes. When I was in grade school I was in Special Education classes. She was the teacher who pulled me out of class and helped me one-on-one. She taught me a lot of the important things like personal hygiene and self-confidence, which were important life lessons and she was there to teach them to me. Now I look back and am grateful for these special women in my life.

As a mentor it is sometimes challenging to set aside your own work or home distractions as well as your "quick solutions" or judgments about her behavior. You are there to listen carefully with an open heart so she feels respected and acknowledged. You are building a relationship with a girl who is missing a positive female role model in her life. Baby steps are required to be worthy of her trust. As a mentor, you are taking the time to allow her to get her thoughts, dreams, upsets and ideas out into the safe space that you have made available to her. You are allowing her to be heard—an amazing, spectacular gift that you can give and that your mentee can receive when she is ready.

Here are some other questions to ask yourself to help you determine if you are mentor material:

- Will you keep conversations confidential?
- Can you be an adult friend, not a parent?
- Can you refrain from psychoanalyzing her?
- Are you comfortable with a girl who has a very different background than your own?
- Are you a good, nonjudgmental listener?
- Are you willing to be playful and have fun?
- Do you have a positive attitude?
- Are you willing to be supportive?
- Can you be patient while your relationship blossoms over time?

I don't know about you, but I have a rather powerful "Mama Bear" inside of me that wants to solve problems and protect the innocent! As a mentor, my role must be neutral yet supportive. We are not there to get to the bottom of a problem—emotionally or otherwise. We are there to listen, care and pay attention. These are powerful gifts to offer.

A Dozen Reasons to Mentor

Yesterday, I heard a gifted high school teacher invite her students to volunteer at a local free food program. She told them, "We don't give a hand out, we give a hand UP!" As a mentor to a girl, you may be giving her a hand up, but the mentoring relationship positively affects many other people in her life and her community. Mentoring is definitely not a "one way street." The love goes both ways! Here are twelve reasons to mentor that you may not have thought about.

1. **Pay it forward.** Think about the adults that supported, encouraged and had your best interests in mind when you were growing up. There are millions of children and teenagers that would love to benefit from your life experience. Mentors give the gift of time and attention. Self-esteem and confidence blossom in those conditions.

2. **Share your skills.** As a mentor you have the unique opportunity to share your skills with a young person. Show her how to cook a meal, read an analog clock or learn map-reading skills. Ask her what she wants to learn to do. Help her with her homework or help her style her hair.

3. **Let her be the teacher.** Letting a girl teach you a card game, make a lanyard bracelet or load music on your new MP3 player are huge boosts to her self-confidence because you are showing her that you respect her own skills and abilities.

4. **Learn to be a child again.** Making time to have fun, be silly and laugh is severely underrated in our adult lives. You'll be pleased

to find out that riding a merry-go-round, singing along to songs on the radio or playing Go Fish! can be quite relaxing and stress-reducing. See the world through a child's eyes!

5. **Practice being a role model.** When a girl is looking up to you week after week and begins to reflect on what you've said or something you did, it is both a compliment and a reminder to you. Children do pay attention to the adults in their lives—even though it's not always apparent. They listen to the choices you present and, believe it or not, they sort through them when they have to make a difficult decision. Don't ever forget that just by showing up and listening, you are an important part of your mentee's life, whether she is telling you or not.

6. **Be your mentee's personal cheerleader.** Whether it's reminding her of her wonderful qualities as a person, the good grades she's gotten at school or attending her school music concert, your positive presence makes a huge impact. Mentors have a unique role in the life of a child; we are all about support, encouragement and really hearing what she has to say. This is a unique and special relationship for two people to share—whatever the age.

7. **Feel good about your contribution to your community.** There are far more children wanting a positive adult role model in their lives than there are adults willing to volunteer. Your commitment of time and attention can literally rewrite the future of a child. Be proud of what you are doing and know that in time, when trust is building, you will hear how important you are to this little girl.

8. **Learn about yourself in your mentoring relationship.** Sometimes adults become mentors because they think they've got life "all figured out" and can tell a child "how it's done." But when you learn about the peer pressure and substance abuse that children deal with in school, let alone the challenges they face in their family life, you realize you cannot "fix" things for this child in all cases. Learning to listen and support in a nonjudgmental manner are powerful skills—lessons and gifts that mentoring makes possible.

9. **You're like Ghandi: "Be the change you want to see in the world."** You not only noticed young girls around you growing up too fast and/or making poor choices about boys, sex or clothing, but you decided to do something about it. You stepped forward to get involved and be part of the solution. Bravo!

10. **You are demonstrating to other adults that they too can make a difference.** Deciding to reshuffle your priorities and reallocate your time does not occur in a vacuum. Other people notice— your friends, coworkers, neighbors and family members! Just hearing you say, "Monday's my night for mentoring" catches the attention of others, causing them to think about how they spend their own time and whether it is time well spent. You're an inspiration to others!

11. **You are helping a parent or guardian to protect their child.** Many parents and guardians are truly struggling to be decent parents along with the many other challenges they face. As a mentor to their child, you could provide the peace of mind the parent (not to mention the child) has been seeking desperately for a long time. Their gratitude may or may not be expressed, but your contribution will not go unnoticed.

12. **Make a new friend.** True friends don't have to be your age. By spending time with a child or teenager, you will see the world from her perspective, which can be very refreshing. Your weekly time together will make both of your lives a little bit sweeter.

Chelsea says...

You are a mentor every day of your life whether you realize it or not. People are looking up at you at any point all the time, whether you are a mother, whether you are a sister, whether you are an only child all by yourself, sitting in a shack. When you leave your house, some person looks up to you at some place. And if you're on the fence about being a mentor, just remember all those smiles that you get during the day. When you open the door for somebody, or when somebody asks you a question at the grocery store, whether you realize it, you're mentoring them.

Final Thoughts

Think back to when you were a girl. Do you remember feeling disappointed when your mom or dad or grandparent had to cancel some plans that you had really been looking forward to? Even after all these years, you may be able to remember what it was, who it was with and exactly how you felt.

Now imagine if that happened continuously. You are constantly being disappointed by the adults in your life. You don't understand why it keeps happening and you start believing you did something wrong and you don't deserve good things or reliable, trustworthy people in your life. Now imagine if you had never known one or both of your parents—let alone your grandparents. Maybe you lived with a single parent but she was too busy to spend time with you. Maybe you lived in the foster care system most of your life. Imagine being a child and all you really wanted was an adult to consistently be there for you, an adult to unconditionally care for you, an adult to always listen to you, an adult who looks forward to seeing you and is interested in what you have to say.

There are thousands of children who go to bed every night and dream of meeting such an adult. But it is just a dream because there aren't enough adults who have decided that they have something to contribute to a child. If you are reading this book, you have something to contribute to a child! You could make a child's dream come true by becoming a mentor.

In the chapters ahead I will make every effort to prepare you to be a great mentor and to help the youth mentoring movement. Chapter 2 shows you how to make time for mentoring. In chapters 3 and 4, I share how to identify the best mentoring opportunity for you and how to begin building your relationship with your mentee. In chapter 5, I cover a variety of practical issues (cultural differences, liability and health issues, relating to the adults in her life) that you may encounter so you know what to do. Chapter 6 talks about how to build confidence in your mentoring skills and I offer tips and tools that will help your mentoring light shine. Chapter 7 talks about building your mentee's self-confidence and provides some stories that show Chelsea's evolving self-confidence throughout the years of our mentoring relationship. Chapter 8 offers a number of tools and techniques for "when the going gets tough," and I relate some stories of tough times with Chelsea and the lessons we both learned. A variety of activity ideas and exercises are made available in chapter 9 and chapter 10 focuses on how women can help get great men involved in mentoring boys.

Reflection: What Are Your Reasons to Be a Mentor?

Take a look at the "A Dozen Reasons to Mentor" table on the following page.

- Which reason(s) really speak to you? Place an "X" in front of them.
- Which reason(s) can you add to the list?

A Dozen Reasons to Mentor
(Add your own too!)

	X	Reasons to Mentor
1		Pay it forward.
2		Share your skills.
3		Let her be a teacher.
4		Learn to be a child again.
5		Practice being a role model.
6		Be your mentee's personal cheerleader.
7		Feel good about your contribution to your community.
8		Learn about yourself in your mentoring relationship.
9		You're like Ghandi: "Be the change you want to see in the world."
10		You are demonstrating to other adults that they too can make a difference.
11		You are helping a parent or guardian to protect their child.
12		You will make a new friend.
13		
14		
15		
16		

CHAPTER TWO

You Can Make Time for Mentoring

With time and patience the mulberry leaf becomes a silk gown.
—Chinese Proverb—

Most formal mentoring programs will ask you for a year's commitment. Trust between a mentor and mentee is not built quickly—it needs time. In the case of children who have been let down by adults so many times, trust needs to be earned.

Knowing that a year's commitment might be required, you are no doubt coming up with all kinds of reasons as to why you can't be a mentor, chief of which is that you don't have time! I feel ya sister! Back in late spring of 2000, Jennifer Granholm, Michigan's then attorney general and now former governor, was invited to speak at my church about the state's "2000 Mentors in the Year 2000" campaign. At that time in my life, I had taken an Educational Leave of Absence from my employer and I was finishing up a much-delayed graduate school degree at the University of Michigan-Dearborn. I was dating a man with a ten-year-old daughter who lived with him fifty percent of the time, and was trying to get comfortable with being part of their little family and routine. In addition, I was about six months into a three-year study of Improvisational Theatre at the Second City Comedy Theatre Training

Center in Detroit. I had lots of friends through an outdoorsy, social club called SOLAR and we liked to do active things and hang out on a regular basis. I enjoyed having a flexible schedule around my time in school, improvisation classes, my friends and my relationship with Harvey, especially in regards to travel. My parents were fairly healthy and aging gracefully and split their time between Grand Rapids, Michigan and Naples, Florida depending on the season. I stayed in touch with my three siblings who lived in Michigan or Florida. My life was squarely based in the southeast Michigan area and I was busy socially, creatively and academically. In other words, I already had a full life—very full. When I first heard about mentoring, in fact, one of my first thoughts was, "How would I ever be able to fit yet another commitment into my world?" I mean, I had to choose my priorities!

During the next several Sundays following the Granholm visit, the senior minister talked to the congregation about getting involved as volunteers in the church and other causes that mattered, especially in youth mentoring. I learned that the youth mentoring programs were looking for adults that could make at least a one-year commitment to devote time weekly to a child. Consistency was really important in these programs since the typical child normally did not have a reliable adult in his or her life.

At first, I was alternately intrigued by and terrified of the idea. A year? Weekly meetings? It seemed like a huge commitment. Would I be able to stick with such a huge commitment? I'd often thought of volunteering, but had seldom done much about it. Besides, I valued the flexibility in my current life; I liked coming and going as I pleased and wondered if I would feel overly tied down by a weekly schedule. And what if "my" child came from a really troubled family? How would I handle that?

On the other hand…this was an opportunity to make a difference in a child's life, and it might even be fun. Would I be able to work with a boy or girl? I remembered all the fun things I did as a child and the new activities like camping, mountain biking and inline skating I had learned as an adult. How much more fun would it be to share these things with a young person, and maybe even teach "my mentee" how to do them? Slowly, curiosity was winning over pessimism.

While I dealt with my internal struggle over the idea of mentoring, my friend Deb jumped right in and met her mentee, a fourteen-year-old boy. She wasn't the only one from our church; five hundred other adults from my church had come forward as well. Wow! The pressure was on.

How Much Time?

Depending on the type of mentoring program you choose (more about that in the next chapter) you will spend between one and two hours a week on average, not including travel time. Weekly meetings are typically the norm to build trust and a solid relationship. I can assure you that you will enjoy this break from your busy job and life.

Here's the time that I allotted over the years to various mentoring programs:

- In my community-based mentoring role, I saw Chelsea on the same night each week from about 6 p.m. – 9 p.m., including travel time and a meal. This fit my work schedule. We met year round with the exception of occasional schedule conflicts or personal vacations.
- When I was a faith-based mentor, I met with the high school teens once a week for two hours. This did not include my travel time to and from the church. Occasionally I accompanied a group to an event on a weekend.
- As a youth ministry teacher/mentor for seventh and eighth graders, I cotaught with another teacher every Sunday for about one hour. Occasionally I accompanied a group to an event on a weekend.
- As a school-based Teen Leadership Coach/Mentor, we met twice a month during the third period, which was less than one hour.
- When I helped out with an occasional Challenge Day program at a local middle school or high school, the program started at

7:45 a.m. and finished at about 3:30 p.m. There was some extra time built in at the beginning and end to prepare/debrief the volunteers.

- In my mentor/tutor role at a local charter school, I met with my student for one hour every week while school was in session. This did not include my travel time.

Some mentoring programs take place during a school's lunch period. You may meet with your mentee in the cafeteria where you eat your lunches together and your together time might only be thirty minutes on a weekly basis.

Most mentors devote a total of nine months to one year in a planned or formal mentoring program. Allotting this amount of time is absolutely critical to building trust and a solid relationship with your mentee. Think about this very carefully: your mentee is either completely missing a female role model or the relationship with their female role model is at least unstable She needs stability over time with you. She needs to know that you will not disappear like other women have in her life.

Equally important is the quality of that time. Put yourself in the shoes of a girl who is missing a dedicated female parent, guardian or role model in her life—someone who cares, listens and guides her when she needs it and even when she doesn't think she needs it. She craves quality time with a special woman who will help build her self-esteem and show her "You are important to me!" Quality time is a critical, important and necessary gift that every girl deserves and requires to develop. You can give her that gift as her mentor.

Chelsea says...

With Paula there was not one time when she didn't call ahead of time if she was unable to make it. Even when she was a few minutes late, she would call to let me know, "I'm on the highway; I'll be a little late." That shows effort. That showed me that she cared.

How to Make Time for Mentoring:
Reprioritization, Flexibility and Thinking Differently

Have you ever heard the saying: If you want something done well, give it to a busy person? It's true! Busy women can pack a lot of things into their days, weeks or months. We set our priorities, manage our time and juggle a lot of things quite well thank you very much. Whether you have a part-time or full-time job, are head of the family household, are retired and/or attend school (or are involved in your children's or grandchildren's school activities), you can make time in your schedule to mentor a child.

Making time for mentoring requires a different way of thinking, some flexibility and reprioritizing. Instead of thinking about mentoring as adding something extra to your very full schedule, view it as incorporating a child into some of your existing activities, such as running errands, having dinner, exercising or doing sports. You will get things done—with her help—and she will feel like she is an important part of your life. By incorporating her into your routine, you can connect and build a relationship. Your mentoring time does not have to be costly and extra-special week after week; in fact that sends the wrong message. Your presence is the "present." Your time and attention is what is special to her. Things and distractions do not a relationship make; people and quality time do.

Reprioritizing Your Time

We all have the same amount of time in a day. But how do you use yours? Are you always answering to the demands of others or are you choosing to make a contribution to a person who needs your help? While we can't "make time," we can choose to reprioritize how we spend our time. I realize you don't have a first-hand opinion on the value of a mentoring relationship like I do. But I can assure you it is time well spent; you will become one of the most important adults in a little girl's life.

Time Management: Communication and Calendars

When you are matched with a young person, as the relationship grows so will the dependency. It is important to have up-front discussions with the parent or guardian and child regarding availability of both you and the young person you are mentoring. Setting up a regular time when you are both free to meet and spend quality time together is a good start. The key is to set parameters so that you can take care of yourself and the important people in your life, yet still allot some quality time to your mentee.

Once you both commit to a time schedule, it is important that the schedule remains consistent throughout the mentoring relationship. It will take time to develop a relationship—trust me—and the first several weeks are crucial in assuring the child that you will be available on a consistent basis. Trust is the foundation upon which the relationship will grow and evolve.

Communicating with your mentee and her family to set up and confirm times is where flexibility comes in handy. In this age of technology, the lines of communication are always open through e-mail, voice mail, and text messaging either with the parent or guardian or perhaps even with your mentee. Set clear boundaries as to when your mentee can contact you at home and establish the best time to contact her since she may have after-school projects, homework assignments, and other activities that make her unavailable.

While the time you spend with your mentee will depend largely on your schedule and that of the child and the family members with whom she lives, it may be affected by the level of "buy-in" from the parent or guardian and how well they check the calendar! On occasion, I showed up at Chelsea's house and no one was home! She may have forgotten that it was our night together, or the errands her grandmother was running with the grandkids took longer than expected. I made sure I had everyone's phone number so I could check the status if there ever was a mix up.

It's a good idea to get the child a calendar and make sure she is keeping it up to date. Depending on her age, you may want to coordinate schedule changes with the adult at home, in addition to scheduling directly with your mentee. Chelsea was over eleven years old when we began our mentoring adventure. Her dad put her in charge of the agreed-upon mentor schedule and then removed himself from the equation. He wanted to teach her some responsibility, which was fine with me, and he had many demands on his time. However, for a good year or two, if I had a conflict on one of our regular evenings, I gave him a reminder call in addition to explaining the time conflict to Chelsea. It was my way of making sure her dad was fully informed and there were no surprises.

As an aside, people in your life will wonder what you are doing when you can't accept their invitation because it's your scheduled night to be with your mentee. Rather than keep it a deep, dark secret, tell them what it's like to spend time with a girl on a regular basis. Although keeping personal details confidential is required, sharing the funny moments, the meaningful events and the things you do together is always appropriate. You might be speaking to a mentor wannabe!

Chelsea says...

(Chelsea reflects on the future and mentoring) It's going to be Monday nights for the rest of my life, 'til one of us passes away.

Final Thoughts

There is a huge selection of mentoring programs to fit your lifestyle and your preferred level of involvement. As long as you are willing to make a commitment to a child, on a consistent basis, there is something for everyone. Your willingness to donate your time and attention speaks volumes about the person you want to be. As the Chinese Proverb said at the beginning of this chapter, with time and patience the mulberry leaf becomes a silk gown. Through mentoring, you are making more "silk gowns" possible.

In the next chapter, "Getting Started as a Mentor," I will help you choose the mentoring program that is best for you and advise you on how to make a smooth transition into your important new role.

Reflection: Time

Spend some time with the following questions:

1. Who gave you the gift of quality time when you were growing up? Why was it special?

    _____

    _____

    _____

2. If you didn't receive the gift of quality time from someone special, how often did you wish you had such a person?

    _____

    _____

    _____

3. What day of the week looks good for getting together with your mentee?

    _____

    _____

    _____

4. What time of day would work well in your schedule for mentoring?

    _____

    _____

    _____

CHAPTER THREE

Getting Started as a Mentor

We ask ourselves, who am I
to be brilliant, gorgeous, talented, and fabulous?
Actually, who are you <u>not</u> to be?
—Marianne Williamson—

ack in chapter 2 our story left off with my friend Deb jumping
into mentoring with both feet and me on a stressful guilt trip.
Five hundred volunteers had stepped forward and—truth be
told—I was filled with angst about whether I could fill the shoes of a
mentor. Somewhere between my guilty state and "I might have SOME-
THING to offer...," curiosity won over caution and insecurity. I reluc-
tantly called the church one afternoon to see if they were still looking
for interested adults. "Yes!" I was told enthusiastically, which brought
a wave of mixed feelings to the surface for me. I later picked up some
preliminary paperwork, which turned out to be a lengthy application.
I learned this was going to involve a criminal history check! Suddenly
I felt like my worthiness as a mentor-wannabe was in the spotlight.
What if I didn't pass muster? What would that feel like? How clean did
my record have to be? I knew I had several past speeding tickets on
my driving record—would that put the kibosh on things? There were
fill-in-the-blank areas on the application where I was asked to explain
why I wanted to be a mentor, what I could contribute to a child, and

other thought-provoking questions. Looking at all of these questions, I started to get a little panicked. It was like I was applying for a job, but I had little or no job experience. Suddenly I felt underqualified. "Who the heck am I?" a little voice in my head kept shouting. I was marriage-free, dependent-free and hardly saw my own nieces and nephews. I didn't even want to own a pet because the commitment would disrupt my lifestyle too much! And there I was, trying to prove my "mentor worthiness" in this multipage application.

I decided to treat it as "not that important" in case I was rejected. After all, I was a busy, successful, single woman. I didn't need to be a mentor to prove that I was worthy to myself or others…did I? I sent the paperwork into the Circuit Court system sometime in August 2000 and began counting the days until I got THE NOTICE.

In late September, I received an invitation for the Mentors Plus Volunteer Orientation program scheduled for November 2000. I made the cut! I found that I was feeling quite pleased; perhaps I had wanted this more than I thought. I marked the mid-November date on my calendar, but caution won out again as I reminded myself that I was still checking this out—going to the orientation didn't mean I had to sign one day a week of my life away.

The orientation was a half-day event on a Saturday in Pontiac, Michigan and I was one of about ten volunteers present. As I recall, there were more women than men and most of us were between forty and fifty years of age. The orientation was led by Candy Hlivka and Garry Pullins, who were both connected to the Oakland County Circuit Court system. Candy worked with the Intervention kids—those that had already had a brush with the law and were living in a juvenile facility in the area. Garry worked with the Prevention kids—children considered at risk that were involved in the Youth Assistance programs in the schools to help keep them on the right track. They showed a few videos about the program and explained what mentoring was about. After listening to them describe each of the programs, I decided to work with a child in the Prevention program since the concept of working with the Intervention kids intimidated me.

We heard about the "typical child" in each of the programs, and I learned that even wealthy Oakland County had many lower income cities with children that needed mentors. We heard about what these children may have been through in their short childhoods (home environment, parental involvement, number of siblings, challenges) and how these challenges may affect their behaviors and choices as they grow up. The theme that kept surfacing was this: These kids need a dependable, consistent, positive, adult influence in their lives. They need to know someone cares about them. They need to know that you're there for them. I found myself alternately getting drawn in and then getting worried about my role as a mentor.

They went on to tell us that we might really disagree with the kind of home environment we see when we pick up or drop off the child; this was not our concern to take on because we were there for the child. We were told that the child's hygiene or clothes might be less than we would expect—this could not distract us from the child. In fact, it was stressed that our most important role was to be that of a listener and not a judge. If the child wants to talk—let her. If she does not, don't ask probing questions—the child will talk if and when she is ready.

I wondered if I could handle keeping my mouth shut when I saw a problem. Could I just turn away? At the same time I was leery about taking on this kid, I found myself wanting to defend "my child" from the challenges she faced before I even completed the orientation! In other words, I was getting hooked.

We "Mentor Newbies" were given basic guidelines, rules of conduct, and the general expectations of the children and their families. We also heard about the challenges and the rewards of mentoring. We learned that, in Oakland County, only same-sex pairings are made because of the liability issues that could surface. I would definitely be working with a girl. I found out that there is a great need for more men to get involved since there are so many boys needing a consistent male figure in their lives. We were given a list of places to go or things to do that were free; this program wasn't about spending money, it was about spending time with the child.

If there was one thing all the facilitators stressed, it was this: You can't imagine how important a dependable and caring adult in a child's life can be! I think that is when I decided that I wanted to be that person for a child in Oakland County. I could be dependable and caring, and I'd figure out one day at a time how to spend time with the child.

Even though I left the orientation eager to start right away, five months went by before I was paired with my mentee, Chelsea. I tried to be patient, but I felt like an expectant mom without the pregnancy and no guarantee!

While I waited, I was given some background information on Chelsea by Jill, the Youth Assistance contact who was connected to Chelsea's school district. As it turned out, I was not Chelsea's first mentor. Chelsea's original mentor was facing availability issues and the case worker wasn't completely sure if a new mentor was needed for Chelsea or not. Jill wanted to tread softly so there was the least amount of disruption for Chelsea. Chelsea was eleven years old at that time and was in fifth grade. I found out she had repeated fourth grade and thus was a year older than her age group. Her parents divorced when she was nine years old, and she, her father and three siblings lived about fifteen minutes from my house. Jill prepped Chelsea and her dad for a meeting and I was to meet her at Chelsea's home in late April, 2001. Reality struck me one day—I was going to be a mentor in just a few more months! I was getting excited!

How to Make an Informed Decision about Mentoring

Just as with other important decisions in your busy life, I highly recommend doing a little bit of research before committing to a mentoring program. You want to choose the right mentoring "fit" to avoid breaking the heart of a little girl because you went in "blind." To help you collect the information that will be helpful in investigating and selecting a mentoring program, I have provided some steps to guide you through the process. Please put them to good use!

Step 1

Figure Out What Day Works
and Make the Commitment

The year-long commitment I just spoke of will undoubtedly entail a weekly visit with your mentee of between one and three hours on average. Occasionally visits may be less frequent, but weekly is typical and the best scenario to build your mentoring relationship. Look at your calendar right now (or your answers to the questions at the end of chapter 2). What day of the week looks good for getting together with your mentee? Write it down on the worksheet below.

Pick a Day and Make the Commitment

List day(s) you can schedule weekly time with your mentee in rank order (#1 being the very best):

1. Day: _____ Time: _____

2. Day: _____ Time: _____

3. Day: _____ Time: _____

Step 2

Decide Which Type of Mentoring Speaks to You

Mentoring programs come in different flavors: planned (formal) or natural (informal). I chose to get started in a formal, community-based program that was promoted through my church, but you can pick your flavor based on the type of mentoring experience you desire, how much structure you prefer, how well you want to get to know your mentee and how much time you are willing to contribute to the mentoring effort. To help you decide, the following paragraphs describe the two types of mentoring.

Planned or Formal Mentoring

Planned or formal mentoring is done through community-based nonprofit organizations (e.g., Big Brothers Big Sisters or Girl Scouts), places of worship, schools and after-school programs that have established programs and procedures. While Big Brothers Big Sisters is an international organization with locations in every major city, there are also many smaller, local organizations to choose from. Formal mentoring programs generally include a screening process, an orientation and/or training program and certain guidelines for mentors to follow. Guidelines will cover the time commitment, the schedule expected of you, and either provide the program "agenda" or give you a list of suggested activities to do with your mentee.

Community-based programs (where a mentor picks up the mentee at home) are the most flexible in terms of how you spend your time together. I got involved in mentoring through a community-based program called "Mentors Plus" which is part of the Oakland County Youth Assistance program within the Circuit Court Family Division of Oakland County, Michigan. My primary experience as a mentor comes from this community-based mentoring experience. School or church-based programs may have specific curriculum or objectives to follow based on the overall purpose of the sponsoring institution. Mentors may or may not be responsible for coming up with ideas and activities when working with children and more than one adult may be involved in a leadership/mentoring role if it is based in a school or church. You need to ask questions of the program coordinator and decide which one fits you best.

These organizations strive to match positive adult role models with school-aged children who may be from a single-parent home or who don't live with their parents, are having trouble in school or with social skills, or may have gotten in trouble with the law and are in a juvenile detention facility. Children needing a caring adult in their lives are referred to the mentoring organizations by many different sources: school counselors, churches, law enforcement and therapists just to name a few. Sometimes family members may contact organizations directly because they feel the child needs extra intervention or because a same-sex adult role model is missing at home. The common denominator is this: A child is at risk and needs an extra caring adult to step in and provide positive influence and direction before it's too late or more poor decisions are made. This is where the miracles can begin! Later in this chapter you will find a comprehensive table that provides detailed information about various types of formal mentoring programs.

Natural or Informal Mentoring

You may be an experienced informal mentor already. Are you a favorite aunt to your nieces and nephews? Do the neighborhood kids like to play in your backyard, and do you like to spend time with them? Do you seem to have a natural comfort level with young people and enjoy talking to them when waiting in line at Starbucks or across the checkout counter at the grocery store? That's what informal mentoring is about — connecting with young people with caring and consideration.

Natural or informal mentoring is much more casual in nature and opportunities may show up in your neighborhood, in your immediate or extended family, with your own children's friends or where you shop or visit in your community. Informal mentoring opportunities may include sports or recreation programs or wherever young people interact with adults who have their best interests in mind. Mentoring could simply be chatting with a young person in any setting — it's about connecting with him or her, giving them positive attention, giving them a compliment, a positive example, feedback, time and attention. It's about making an effort to show your respect and interest in a young person, wherever the opportunity arises. It could be quite spontaneous or even a weekly Friday night movie get-together at your house with some young people you know. It's whatever you decide to create because you like to connect with kids!

What Type of Formal Mentoring Program Speaks to You?

If formal mentoring speaks to you, there are many programs to choose from. Take a moment to review the table on the following pages that provides a comparison of formal mentoring programs. Which type of formal mentoring program interests you? Would you rather set your own weekly "agenda" with your mentee, or would you rather help out with a program that already has activities planned with children at a particular location? Do you want to spend quality one-on-one time with one child or many children? Would you rather be a mentor via the Internet?

After reviewing the table on the next few pages, choose the type of formal program(s) that appeals to you. Circle the mentoring program characteristics that sound interesting. Circle the type of program you prefer in one of the columns (e.g., community-based, faith-based, etc.) as a reminder.

The type of formal mentoring program that is attractive to me is:

1. _____

   Why? _____
   _____
   _____
   _____

2. _____

   Why? _____
   _____
   _____
   _____

A Comparison of Formal Mentoring Programs **

	Community-based	School-based	After-school	Faith-based	Special Populations	Work & Service-based
Program Type	Big Brothers, Big Sisters, other local programs	Reading program; Math tutoring; Life Skills Mentoring Programs; Challenge Day (CD) programs	Latchkey; YMCA; Boys & Girls Club	Sunday school; possible collaboration with justice systems and/or social services	Juvenile facilities; Advanced Placement programs in high schools; Runaway Shelters; Children of Prisoners etc.	Paid employment; unpaid internships; service-learning; Junior Achievement
Program Purpose	Positive adult role model for child; social activities	Student needs more personalized help with school work; social skills; life skills; positive adult role model; violence prevention (CD)	Recreation; tutoring; supervision after school	Youth Ministry, spiritual principles, values clarification; link high risk youth with positive adult role models	Positive adult role model; special studies and training; adult friend; life skills	**Work/Internships:** Informal and formal paid/unpaid employment experiences for youth **Service-learning:** Activities that combine specific educational purposes with the aim of benefiting others **Junior Achievement:** Inspire and lead young people to succeed in a global environment. Adults volunteer to help youth learn business skills
Typical Mentee	Single parent home; emotionally at-risk child; low income (there are exceptions to this "rule")	Academically at-risk child; gifted youth; diverse student populations (CD)	"Latchkey" kids; single parent homes; neighborhood kids	Cross section of all socio-economic backgrounds connected to that faith community; high risk youth, neglected or abused youth, runaways	Juvenile offenders; talented youth; pregnant/parenting adolescents; abused and neglected youth; runaways; youth with disabilities; children of prisoners	School-aged youth (age depends on program)

A Comparison of Formal Mentoring Programs **

	Community-based	School-based	After-school	Faith-based	Special Populations	Work & Service-based
Child's Gender	Same-gender matches	Both	Both	Both	Depends on population/program	Both
Solo or Group Meeting	Solo	Both	Both	Both	Both	Both
Frequency	Weekly	Weekly/flexible/as-needed	Weekly	Weekly	Weekly	Weekly
Time Commitment	1-4 hours per month (plus travel time)	1+ hours per week (plus travel time); full school day (CD)	1+ hours per week (plus travel time)	1+ hours per week (plus travel time)	1+ hours per week (plus travel time)	1+ hours per week (plus travel time)
Screening Process	Yes (find out what is involved)	Yes (find out what is involved); none for CD	Yes (find out what is involved)	Yes (find out what is involved)	Yes (find out what is involved)	Yes (find out what is involved)
Orientation/Training	Yes	Yes	Yes	Yes	Yes	Yes
Structured or Flexible Program	Flexible (Mentor is in charge of activities)	Structured (working with school staff and academic guidelines); Structured (working with CD Leaders)	Structured (working within program guidelines and/or facility)	Structured/flexible (working within faith-based program guidelines)	Structured/flexible (working with program staff and program guidelines)	Structured/flexible (work within program guidelines)
Location of Mentoring	Community (you decide)	School building	School; YMCA; Boys & Girls Club etc.	Place of worship; community	Community; program facility	Work settings, school settings; Junior Achievement facilities
Who Plans the Time Together	Mentor and mentee	School staff and mentors; Challenge Day Leaders	Program staff and mentors	Faith-based staff and mentors	Program staff and mentors	Program staff and mentors
Year-round Program	Yes	School-year	School-year	Yes	Possible	Possible
Overnight Stays	Check with program	Check with program	Check with program	Check with program	Check with program	Check with program

A Comparison of Formal Mentoring Programs **						
	Community-based	School-based	After-school	Faith-based	Special Populations	Work & Service-based
Contact with Mentee Family	Yes	Possible	Possible	Yes	Possible	Possible
Support for Mentor	Check with program	Check with program	Check with program	Yes	Yes	Check with program
Program Cost	Possible processing cost; meals; tickets etc.	No (unless you bring a treat or special supplies)	No (unless you bring a treat or special supplies)	No (unless you bring a treat or special supplies)	No (unless you bring a treat or special supplies)	No (unless you bring a treat or special supplies)
Opportunity to Connect on a Personal Level with Child	High	Medium; High (CD)	Low-Medium	Low-High	Low-High (depending on population)	Medium-High

** This table may not accurately represent all programs that fall into these categories.

Always research a mentoring program in advance of getting involved so there are no surprises and no disappointments.

Step 3

Research the Mentoring Opportunities Available to You

You may already be aware of mentoring opportunities at the local school, your place of worship, perhaps your workplace or an organization within your community. Even if you are aware, I invite you to review the table on page 62 entitled "Mentoring Resources: How to Get Started Mentoring a Girl." The first resource listed is the MENTOR/ National Mentoring Partnership—a wonderful resource! You can visit their website at www.mentoring.org to really get a full understanding of what is available to you.

Beyond the MENTOR/National Mentoring Partnership information, I have also provided one other international-scale mentoring organization which coordinates Internet-based mentoring between school children and career professionals.

Research the Available Mentoring Opportunities

Using the worksheet on the following page, write down at least three organizations that sounded interesting to you and the contact information. Jot down notes about <u>why</u> they sound interesting based on your research.

1. Review the table on page 62: "Mentoring Resources: How to Get Started Mentoring a Girl."
2. Visit one or more websites. Which programs do you prefer?
3. Write your top three choices on the next page with a phone number and contact name:

A. Program name: _____
    Phone number: _____
    Contact person: _____
    Why it sounds interesting: _____

    _____

    _____

    _____

B. Program name: _____
    Phone number: _____
    Contact person: _____
    Why it sounds interesting: _____

    _____

    _____

    _____

C. Program name: _____
    Phone number: _____
    Contact person: _____
    Why it sounds interesting: _____

    _____

    _____

    _____

Mentoring Resources: How to Get Started Mentoring a Girl

Name of Organization	Purpose of Organization (Information from their website)	Contact Information	Website
MENTOR/ National Mentoring Partnership	MENTOR is the lead champion for youth mentoring in the United States. We serve young people between the ages of six and eighteen, and MENTOR's work over the last two decades has helped millions of young people find the support and guidance they need to build productive and meaningful lives. Currently, eighteen million children in the United States want and need a mentor, and three million have one. MENTOR's mission is to close that "mentoring gap" so that every one of those fifteen million children has a caring adult in their life. **Our Goal** MENTOR helps children by providing a public voice, developing and delivering resources to mentoring programs nationwide and promoting quality for mentoring through standards, cutting-edge research and state-of-the-art tools. The backbone of mentoring's infrastructure is a growing network of state Mentoring Partnerships that MENTOR has helped to build and support.	(703) 224-2200	www.mentoring.org
International Telementor Program	The International Telementor Program (ITP) facilitates electronic mentoring relationships between professional adults and students worldwide, and is recognized as the leader in the field of academic-based mentoring. Since 1995 over 40,000 students throughout nine countries have received support, encouragement, and professional guidance. ITP serves students in K-12 and home school environments as well as college and university settings. Telementoring is a process that combines the proven practice of mentoring with the speed and ease of electronic communication, enabling busy professionals to make significant contributions to the academic lives of students. Through mentoring by industry professionals, a corporation helps students develop the skills and foundation to pursue their interests successfully and operate at their potential.	E-mail: staff@telementor.org (970) 481-9795 Toll free: 1-877-376-8053 (U.S. and Canada)	www.telementor.org

Step 4

Ask Your Questions and Learn About the Program Requirements

After you've narrowed down which mentoring opportunities you would like to investigate, you'll want to talk to program staff to learn about the programs available. Be open-minded when you speak to these people! Listen to what they have to say and know that they have lots of experience working with children as well as adults just like you. They will probably have recommendations for you based on what you tell them about yourself.

Note: Depending on the size and staffing of the mentoring organization, how a mentee is matched with a mentor, mentor training and ongoing support could be handled very differently. Your goal is to find out as much information about the level of support you will get as a mentor and to figure out if you will be comfortable in that environment. The last thing you want to do is be matched with a child and decide that the organization doesn't meet your needs. These children do not need another adult disappointing them.

Worksheet: Call Mentoring Organizations, Ask Your Questions and Learn about the Program Requirements

1. Decide how many organizations you will research.
2. Make one copy per organization of the worksheet on the following two pages.
3. Let the steps on the worksheet guide your conversation when you contact the organization. Write down some notes on the worksheet so you are clear on what you are looking for and you can share what you have to offer when you talk to the program staff.

PROGRAM NAME: _____

Contact person: _____

1. Explain that you are interested in mentoring one (or more) young people; are they looking for adult volunteers?

   _____

2. Describe the amount of time you have to give, a little bit about your background, any experience you've had with children and the types of activities you are interested in (e.g., teach a specific skill, pursue an interest together, help with homework or just spend quality time together).

3. What types of mentoring opportunities are available (e.g., one-on-one, group, one-time events etc.)?

   _____

   _____

   _____

4. How does the program match a child with an adult? For example:
   - Is there an interview involved for the mentor?
   - Is the child interviewed about her interest in having a mentor?
   - Is the girl receptive to having a mentor?
   - Is the match based on location alone, or do they consider interests or background too?
   - Is the parent or guardian at home supportive of a mentor forming a relationship with their child? (Many are not, but they know—or it's been strongly suggested to them—that it's the right thing to do for the child. This is good background information to know going into the relationship.)

   _____

   _____

   _____

   _____

   _____

5. What type of orientation, training and support is available for volunteers? How frequently do they occur? Is it only at the beginning or are there other educational opportunities available on a regular basis?

_____

_____

_____

_____

_____

6. What does the application process involve?

_____

_____

_____

7. Once I complete the application process, how soon will I get started?

_____

_____

8. Share the locations you are willing to work in.

_____

_____

9. Is there someone I can call if I have a question or concern once I get started?

_____

_____

10. Your own questions:

_____

_____

_____

_____

_____

_____

Step 5

Choose a Program

Mentors are needed NOW! Look at the information you collected in Step 4. Decide which program fits your needs and attracts you the most. Don't delay following through on your decision to become a mentor. The reality is that many adults take the first step, but very few actually follow through. Be the mentor a little girl is waiting for—make her dream come true!

Make a Decision and Take Action Now!

1. Write down which mentoring program appeals to you most and why.

    I prefer this program: _____

    _____

    Why?_____

    _____

    _____

    _____

2. Call the appropriate staff person you spoke to and/or met with TODAY and schedule an appointment to meet and begin the interview/application process.

    Appointment date and time:_____

    _____

Final Thoughts

You've just completed the steps that will help you make a great choice of a mentoring opportunity. In fact, I bet the program directors that you have spoken with will be shocked that you are so well prepared! (You can take all the credit—I don't mind.)

Just do a child a favor and act quickly. She wants you in her life as soon as possible. You want her in your life too—trust me on this. In the next chapter I'll tell you all the things you want to know about getting started in the best possible way. I want you to feel prepared and comfortable in your new role and help you get your "sea legs" while you begin building your relationship.

Success means we go to sleep at night knowing that our talents and abilities were used in a way that served others.
—Marianne Williamson—

CHAPTER FOUR

Your Relationship with Your Mentee: Getting Started on the Right Foot

No one cares how much you know, until they know how much you care.
—*Don Swartz*—

On the agreed-upon day and time, I arrived at Chelsea's home for our first meeting. Jill (the Youth Assistance caseworker) had told me that she would meet me there, and that Chelsea and her dad would be joining us. I sat in my SUV waiting for some adults to show up. Almost immediately, the door of the house opened and a youngish teenage girl looked squarely at me while talking on her phone. She motioned for me to come into the house. "Come in to the house?" I gasped; I felt like I was breaking the rules already as I had been told to wait for the caseworker. But because of this girl's attention (was this Chelsea?) I got out of my SUV and went up to the door. The girl told me, "My dad will be home pretty soon," and continued to talk on the phone.

I mumbled, "I think I'm supposed to wait until your dad gets here," but she pointed to the couch in the living room. "She sure looks mature for eleven years old, and she seems pretty well adjusted too!" I thought, and I asked her, "Are you Chelsea?"

She replied, "No, I'm Sam (as in Samantha)—that's Chelsea!" She pointed to a quiet figure on the couch in the dimly-lit living room. (*Faux pas numero uno!* Talk to the wrong child and completely overlook the girl I'm there to meet!)

I looked at the girl on the couch and introduced myself. "Hi Chelsea, I'm Paula."

"Hi," she said quickly and sat with her hands hidden beneath her thighs.

I felt like an invader and she looked really nervous. I was nervous too! A wonderful beginning…she quietly stared at the floor. My first inclination when I encounter silence is to fill the space with my voice, so I started asking questions that might uncover some common interests. "Do you like to ride your bike?" I asked.

"Yes!" she said.

"Cool!" I thought. I continued, "Do you like to rollerblade?"

"Yes!" she responded.

I was on a roll! I asked some more questions, trying to cleverly anticipate what she might already like to do so I could show that we were truly a match made in Heaven. "Yes!" she replied to each and every question I came up with.

"Hmmm…" I thought. "Is it possible she truly likes to do all the things I asked her about?" Much later, I found out Chelsea would have probably said "Yes!" if I asked her if she'd like to eat worms and cockroaches, since she wanted more than anything to be accepted by me— her replacement mentor. She was still smarting from her first mentor disappearing with little or no explanation, and she didn't want anything to stand in her way.

After an incredibly long fifteen minutes, Chelsea's dad arrived looking harried. The case worker, Jill, called to say she would be delayed. I looked at all the family pictures displayed on the mantle over the fireplace and noticed Chelsea was one of four children in the household. She had an interesting way of smiling in each picture: she put the tip of her tongue between her teeth! (Years later, Chelsea told me that she had seen a movie with the twin child actresses Mary Kate and Ashley and they had smiled that way, which she considered very cool. She had adopted the smile for herself and made sure she demonstrated it in her school pictures for several years in a row.) It was pretty clear her dad certainly had his hands full with four kids at home.

To my intense relief, Jill eventually arrived at the house and made the formal introductions, covered some basic information about the program, and suggested we pick an agreeable time for Chelsea and I to get together each week. Jill left, and I decided it might be good for me and Chelsea to spend a little bit of time together away from her family. I asked Chelsea and her dad if it was okay to take Chelsea down the street to get a soft drink. They both agreed and off we went to the nearest Wendy's. I think we both had lemonade and we talked about when we might meet during the week and what we might do together. This was sort of like interviewing a job candidate or a prospective date, but with a lot less experience on both our parts! Chelsea impressed me as a very polite girl who really wanted to make a good impression. She talked a little bit about school and her family in monosyllabic responses and took frequent sips of her lemonade. She made very little eye contact and seemed excited and nervous all at the same time. Little did she know that I desperately wanted to make the same good impression with her and her dad. The first meeting went well and we planned to include a weekly dinner and an activity on a weekday evening. (What was THAT going to be?)

During our first official evening together, I took her to Logan's restaurant down by the mall near her house. Chelsea ordered a huge hamburger and fries. We were eating dinner and I was making conversation when suddenly she said, "Excuse me! I have to use the rest room!" I pointed her in the right direction and sat waiting for her return.

I waited…and waited…and waited. I was torn between being patient and having paranoid thoughts that she had been kidnapped! Several times I fought the urge to go into the bathroom and ask if she was okay. As I was about to spring into action she came back to the table. Phew!

No sooner had we started eating again when Chelsea said, "Excuse me! I have to use the rest room!" She jumped off the bench and made a beeline for the bathroom! More paranoid thoughts: "Is she sick?" "Do

I make her uncomfortable?" "Should I ask her what's wrong?" You name it, I stressed about it! She returned.

"Chelsea—are you okay?" I asked.

"Yes!" she responded.

We made it through the rest of dinner, but just before we left the restaurant she made yet another beeline to the bathroom. I was perplexed. She seemed alright after she came out of the bathroom, but wasn't willing to say what was going on. I decided not to probe—according to the mentor guidelines—and bit my lip rather than question her further. Two years or so later I finally found out what was going on. The incident came up in conversation, and after two years together I felt confident enough to finally probe a bit. It turns out that she was so nervous that she kept feeling sick. "I was too embarrassed to tell you!" she said. And I thought I was nervous!

Since Chelsea had expressed enthusiasm for outdoor activities when we first met, I tried taking her biking at one of the local parks. When I grabbed Chelsea's bike to load it into the car, I found out it weighed about forty pounds and the tires were gasping for air. Despite not having the best bike for the task, Chelsea forged ahead with me as we wound around the dirt and wood chipped trails. She was a trooper and never complained once, though whenever she saw a park bench she gasped, "Can we sit down?" Maybe biking wasn't her thing, but she was very willing to participate.

We also tried rollerblading. I remember she had pink and white blades and they made a loud noise as the bearings needed some maintenance. I gave her one of my bike helmets to wear as I am a very serious helmet user and I believe everybody should wear one. I gave her some wrist and knee guards, because I was having visions of Chelsea crashing into a tree or going fifty miles per hour down a hill with nothing but a T-shirt and shorts to "protect" her. Chelsea would skate ahead—like she was on a mission from God—with short, quick strides and wear herself out in the process. It seemed that we sat down on every park bench, but that was okay. We were getting some exercise and I was praying that the bonding between us was beginning to happen.

It was hard to tell how Chelsea felt about our budding relationship. She talked a lot about what was going on at school, in her family or in the moment, but she didn't really go much deeper than that. I just let her talk and tried to be an interested, nonjudgmental listener while I learned how to be a mentor. At the Mentor Orientation we were told not to probe, but just let the child talk if and when they were ready. I could do that; Chelsea seemed like a happy girl and I was feeling pretty lucky to have her in my life.

The Moment Has Arrived!

Getting over your new mentor jitters will happen sooner than you think. But your jitters as an adult are minor compared with the jitters that your new mentee is experiencing. In her eyes, you may represent the woman she has always wanted in her life, but is afraid to hope for in case she is disappointed again. She is nervous, excited and scared and she probably didn't sleep a wink last night either! Plus, she's a girl—not a grown-up woman like you.

As stated in *Building Relationships: A Guide for New Mentors* published by the National Mentoring Center (2008):

> While establishing a friendship may sound easy, it often is not. Adults and youth are separated by age and, in many cases, by background and culture. Even mentors with good instincts can stumble or be blocked by difficulties that arise from these differences. It takes time for youth to feel comfortable just talking to their mentor, and longer still before they feel comfortable enough to share a confidence. Mentees cannot be expected to trust their mentors simply because the program staff members have put them together.

Even so, I want you to feel comfortable getting started because I want yours to be a long-term relationship. As with any new relationship, you need to tread softly and take the time that it requires. Be patient and get to know each other. In this chapter you will find some ideas on how to connect with girls, and how to support conversation and when to just listen. I also discuss the many flavors of your role as mentor, some tips on how to be a "Marvelous Mentor" plus some really great "Mentor Guiding Principles" from a good friend of mine.

Preparing for Your First Meeting: Getting In Touch with Girls

Unless you happen to have some girls living with you at home, feeling out of touch with the younger generation makes a lot of sense. When I was considering being a mentor, I was single and a distant aunt to a total of seven nieces. I had worked in a junior high school twenty years prior and the outspoken, irreverent age group freaked me out a bit. I didn't like "girly" things then and I still don't today. So, I can relate if "feeling out of touch" happens to speak to you. But, don't let this stop you. There are many ways you can connect with girls today that will help you warm up to your role as mentor.

Spending a day helping at a local school or at your church are ways to get in touch with girls. Not only will you begin to understand the complexities of girls, the issues they confront and the peer pressure, but more importantly you'll gain understanding of the language and the catch phrases used by this new generation. It doesn't mean you need to adopt the language of girls; it's just helpful to understand it.

Do you have nieces? Spend a day or two with them and listen to the language they use; notice the body language and facial expressions. If you don't quite understand a comment they make or a catch phrase they use, ask for some help! Ask them questions about the latest trends, what's new in school, and how they handle stress and relationships. Talk about interests, music, movies and the latest fads. Chances are they'll think you're pretty cool because you're asking them to be your teacher. What a compliment to them!

When you sign up as a mentor you will be given a comprehensive orientation and/or training session so you feel more comfortable with your new adventure. You might engage in exercises that will give you a better understanding of how to utilize the tools and resources that are open to you, and they'll give you a little practice up front.

The First Meeting

Gaining confidence as a mentor can be analogous to learning how to use the Internet. At first glimpse, the Internet may seem intimidating. If you push the wrong button while you're typing, the information you've worked on for hours is lost. You may feel disoriented as you attempt to navigate different websites, and error messages may leave you at your wits' end. However the more you work at understanding the Internet via tutorials or books and trial and error, you will begin to understand how it works. Eventually you will become so good at navigating the Web that you'll wonder why you hadn't purchased a computer or paid for Internet service earlier.

The same thing can be said for mentors. Upon first meeting, you may feel awkward and not know what to say or do; the mentee may seem quiet and reserved, and you may feel this is not a good match. Remember that the girl you mentor needs your assistance and, as leery as you may be about the situation, the mentee's feelings must supersede your own.

Once the proverbial ice is broken, both you and your mentee will begin to relax and start a conversation. Not everything has to be decided at the first meeting. Discussing general topics is a good place to begin and with each meeting you will become more confident. Remember too that you will have a mentor organization liaison of your own to help you with any problems that may arise. Your contact person would love for you to call whenever you feel the need. Just keep in mind that you're the adult and you're being asked to be a friend to a scared child. It is always easier for you than for the girl sitting next to you. Make a commitment now to see this through. Be an example of a new kind of adult in her life.

How to Keep the Dialogue Rolling

"How was your week Chelsea?"

"Okay..."

"How did that math test go last week?"

Silence.

Even after your relationship with your mentee has become somewhat more established, it will at times be hard to get a conversation going. It could be her mood, what's going on at home, a bad day at school or just exhaustion! It could also be that YOU are tired, feeling cranky, or just not feeling conversational. Expecting an effortless, flowing, balanced dialogue with your mentee may not be completely realistic for a while. However, once she feels comfortable and gets talking you may have a hard time getting two words into the conversation!

While you get to know each other, here are some tips to help you keep the dialogue rolling.

1. **Show Your Interest**: Asking yes/no questions may get you a limited response. To really encourage conversation, show your interest in your mentee and ask follow-up questions to help her share a little bit more information. When she responds, keep the dialogue moving by saying something open-ended and supportive, such as:

    - "Wow! That's great! Tell me more about that."
    - "That sounds really interesting—what did you do next?"
    - "Do you mean...?"
    - "I think I understand—can you give me an example?"
    - "That's so cool! Have you thought about...?"

2. **Be Ready to Answer Yourself:** Don't be surprised if she turns a question around and wants you to answer it! Depending on the topic and her age, being honest goes a long way here, and she'll respect you for your authenticity. Plus, she'll trust you even more for not dodging the questions like most adults do.

3. **Explore Different Topics—Superficial and Deep:** You will be surprised how listening to a song by Kelly Clarkson or Lady Gaga can lead to a deep discussion about how boys treat girls. Every talk doesn't have to be deep, but deep discussions will become more prevalent as the two of you get comfortable with each other. It's all about showing true interest for each other—that's what makes your talks together memorable and meaningful.

4. **Today May Not Be the Day to Talk:** Some days your mentee will be quiet and reserved or maybe even angry or sullen. Although Chelsea was not one to hold back too much when she had something on her mind, the days she was quieter stuck out like a sore thumb! If she turned on the car radio right away, that was typically a sign that she didn't want to talk. If your innocent, "How was your night with your dad?" question seems to be ignored or you get a pointed look, just back off and pick another more superficial topic. When and if she's ready to talk, she'll let you know.

5. **Support Is the Focus, Not Judgment:** At some point, your mentee will share information that may not sit well with you. You may be shocked, disagree or worry about the consequences for her. Keeping the conversation going and keeping your relationship growing is dependent on how you react in these situations. Keep an open mind. Try to understand her perspective—ask questions so you really understand where she's coming from. Find out how she feels and what she is thinking about. You are not there to fix the problem, you are there to support her and not pass judgment.

Chelsea says...

Chelsea shares tips on what keeps communication flowing:

A mentor needs to be open-minded to getting out of her comfort zone. You have to be able to get close to someone.

We both show each other that we care—our relationship is even. It's not just about her and it's not just about me. We have developed a relationship that is mutual. Most friendships are not mutual. We hold each other's hands and don't let go—during challenging times and victories. We have been together for ten years!

Going through stuff in my life like peer pressure and mistakes—I learned so much from having my mentor there and asking me questions. She made me aware of what I was doing.

Know When to Just Sit Back and Listen: Different Approaches to Listening

Now I've given you some tips on how to start a conversation with your mentee and keep it going, I'm going to advise you to stop talking and start listening! Listening is powerful stuff! She's on the "stage" and you are her "audience." She feels important and you're earning trust and respect. It's a win-win situation. Here are some different approaches to listening.

Car Time and Being a Neutral Listener

One of the most important "services" I provide for Chelsea is that of neutral listener. There is something about her climbing into my car and closing the door that causes her to start talking! I'm glad she feels comfortable "venting" when she gets together with me if something is going on in her life. I know she trusts me and feels comfortable talking to me. In fact, it's rather odd if she doesn't start talking immediately—then I REALLY know something is going on. I don't like to start prying right away. I'll just ask harmless questions like, "Did you have a nice weekend?" or, "What have you been up to since I last saw you?" or I'll just compliment her on her hair or her outfit. Usually the most banal questions start the outflow of what's bothering her, or who's bugging her, or what she's been worrying about.

Trust: Accept Her Version at Face Value

A "gift" I try to give Chelsea is to accept her version of the truth at face value. If she wants to revise it or add to that truth at a later time, so be it. That is why I have never tried to befriend any adult member of her family alongside of my relationship with Chelsea. On a few occasions Chelsea's dad sought me out because he was concerned about her safety, so I learned his version of the story first—and Chelsea was aware we had talked before I met with her the next time. But in general, the fact that I listen to Chelsea's version of her life without questioning its validity is something she can bank on every week. I accept her as she is without question.

Because I focused on her and her version of what was happening with her life, I earned her trust. Later in our relationship I found out on occasion that she withheld the complete truth, but she voluntarily contributed what was missing—when she was ready—because she couldn't stand the thought of lying to me. I learned over time that the fact that she was willing to talk to me at all, even after the fact, was a huge compliment to me.

Stay Nonjudgmental

I don't know if this is an aspect of my "real" personality or something I take on specifically in my role as Chelsea's mentor, but I don't go off the deep end easily. I've never gotten really angry with her. I know that

Chelsea says...

When I was being bullied at school, Paula tried to teach me about girl power, that what other people think doesn't matter. She taught me it was more about internal respect. Nobody's opinion should matter except my own.

in order for her to tell me what's going on in her life, I need to maintain some level of neutrality.

Building Her Confidence in You: Where Are You Starting From?

It goes almost without saying that you will need to build your mentee's confidence in you. Chances are she will have trust issues with you and early on in your relationship with your mentee, you will need to establish exactly what these trust issues are. She may not trust that you will keep her confidences in you just that—confidential. She may think that you will be judgmental in your listening, even though you say you won't be judgmental. Or, she may not trust that you will keep your promises. Ignoring these trust issues or getting them wrong may mean that your relationship will get off to a rocky start.

Chelsea's main trust issue with me—and the area in which I needed to build her confidence in me the most—was trusting that I would show up. If I had ignored this issue and not built her confidence in me by paying particular attention to keeping my promises about showing up, it would have been difficult to build our relationship.

When I met Chelsea, her parents had been divorced for about two years. Chelsea and her three siblings lived with their dad. They saw

Chelsea says...

You have to open your heart. There were times when I did not want a mentor—I wanted to push everyone away. But Paula never gave up! She uses different ways to teach me. I know she will not leave. We have trust!

Trust is when a mentor knows a mentee on a personal level. It's about being able to use and share personal experiences. It's about being able to talk about sex and drugs. A mentor is slightly like a parent, but the most important thing is that she lets you speak instead of just telling you what to do. She doesn't take sides and isn't accusing. She remains open to listening to me.

their mom every other weekend and sometimes at school functions. I knew virtually nothing about why this custodial arrangement had been set up and just accepted it. In my limited personal exposure to divorce and child custody, it was usually the mother that had the children. Not so here. It wasn't my business to ask questions and I certainly wasn't going to probe. I learned over time that "something bad" had led to her parents' divorce and that was why the children didn't live with their mother. I also gathered that Chelsea had very guarded and conflicted feelings about her mother. She clearly felt abandoned. Strike one against women.

Before I met Chelsea, I was told by the Youth Assistance caseworker that she had another mentor for about eight months, but the mentor had become unavailable and had abandoned the relationship with little notice and not much forethought. In fact, Chelsea never got an explanation from her former mentor until she bumped into her in a local shopping mall. The woman told her, "I just got too busy." Chelsea was hurt and confused by the experience. Strike two against women.

Since her parents' divorce, Chelsea saw a few different women come in and out of her father's life when he returned to the dating scene. She admits viewing each one of her father's new girlfriends and eventually his second wife (which ended a few years later in divorce) as her next real mother because she wanted one so desperately. She needed and wanted a woman in her life that she could love, trust and who wouldn't leave her.

Chelsea says...

In the past I have had a really hard time connecting with females. I have a really hard time getting close with them. I've been abandoned, hurt by, and taken for granted by every female. But with my friendship with Paula, I've never felt that way. I've never felt betrayed.

Given her history with women, why would she believe I would be any different? If I were in her shoes, I would have been pretty hesitant too! However, I kept showing up, I made sure to alert her when I was late or couldn't make it and I kept listening to what she had to say. I proved myself to be trustworthy over time, which bolstered Chelsea's confidence in me.

What Your Relationship Might Look Like

Mentors are kind of like chameleons—we adjust our outer skin covering depending on what is going on in our mentee's life. One day you are her adult girlfriend that she's hanging out with, singing along to a song you both know. The next time you might be the "mom" mentor because you have a sad, bewildered girl sitting next to you who just needs a hug while she tries to figure out why girls are mean or boys are "stupid." But don't forget your neutral role of just being there to listen, not judge and be open to her experience in the world. Every role you play is important.

Chelsea says...

I didn't ever experiment with drugs to be completely honest with you. I don't want to let Paula down. Sometimes, a lot of people think that when you see someone only once a week, you would think that their opinion wouldn't matter, because they don't see you every day. But, when I've been in situations where I have to make an important decision, her face pops up in my head—before my parents, before my boyfriend—before other people. Her face pops into my head, and I remember how much she loves and cares about me and how disappointed she would be if I made a poor decision.

What Your Role as a Mentor IS

You are there for HER—to enjoy her, to share yourself with her, to experience new places and things with her. You are there to help her learn new skills—if she desires—and to learn about the world through her eyes. You are there to encourage her dreams, to believe in herself and to help her see herself as a good person. You are the sunshine in her life who is always a friend, a confidante and a positive role model.

Meet the adults around her so you know who is interested in her welfare and they know you are looking out for her too. Meet her teachers, her counselors, her grandparents and siblings so they know who you are and they know you have her best interests in mind. Let them know the schedule you have with her and collect phone numbers if appropriate. Share your phone number if it is okay with the mentoring organization and if you feel comfortable doing so.

Getting involved in your mentee's life may be a bit unsettling at times. You are walking into a situation that has taken many years to develop, yet you have no control over the past. What I suggest to you is that you CAN influence this child's present, and most certainly her future because you are willing to get involved in her life right now. Your involvement is such a gift, and you can't imagine now what rewards you both will experience in your mentoring relationship. What did Woody Allen say? "Eighty percent of success is showing up." Trust me; you will make a difference in this child's life—just by showing up and caring for her! Make a commitment to be the adult she can trust.

What Your Role as a Mentor IS NOT

Remember: You are not a mentor to fix, change or rescue this girl. You are not her parent, counselor, minister or rescuer. You are her mentor—a positive role model in her life. There will be times when you could get derailed, distracted and turned off by her circumstances. Judging her home life, the people she lives with or her personal hygiene—in front of her—does her no favors and it gives her the message that you don't approve. Just because your choices are different than the people she lives with cannot distract you from your support of her.

Instead, be proactive in a delicate and respectful way. Does she need a bath when you pick her up? If appropriate, bring her to your house and play "dress up," which involves having her take a bubble bath beforehand, washing her hair and laundering her clothes before she goes home. (Thank you Christine Steele for that idea!) Give her a little "dress up" package to take home, filled with the bath products you introduced to her at your home. Does she have dental hygiene problems? Make popcorn together and talk about how popcorn and other foods can get stuck in teeth and cause discomfort and future cavities. Make dental care a "learning adventure" together. Practice dental hygiene at your home and give her her own toothbrush, toothpaste and dental floss to take home to practice on her own.

Relating as a Mother Figure

I have never been a mother so I can't really relate to that role personally. I admit to finding myself having quite a "Mama Bear" instinct when I feel someone is not being fair to Chelsea or is mistreating her in any way. She has shared some background about her relationships with her mother, stepmother, father and siblings and I sometimes find myself wanting to confront them directly and back her up so they really understand that she is "right" and they are "wrong." But, I know that is not my place as a mentor.

I also know that I was not present to see what happened so I don't have the whole story. I find I am quite biased to Chelsea's version of things—since her version is the one I get—so it is difficult for me to hear of conflicts she encounters without getting protective of her.

I imagine that if I was living in the same house with her and the other family members, I would have more information and perhaps draw different conclusions. But I'm sort of glad I just see my portion of Chelsea's life. It keeps things simple and I remain quite supportive of her in every way.

That's who I really want to be for her—I don't want the rest of the family dynamics (or school or boyfriend dynamics) to distract me. On occasion, Chelsea has chosen to "fess up" when she didn't quite share the whole truth with me regarding one issue or another. But she has told me many times that, "I kept thinking about what we've talked about and I didn't want to disappoint you." I would think that every parent would want to hear their child say that to them!

Relating as a Girlfriend

> ### Chelsea says...
>
> We're friends but we're not equal because I see her as a higher, as an alpha, yet every time that we get together, I teach her something about herself and she teaches me something about myself. So it's an even exchange. It's the coolest relationship. That's how it's different.

Chelsea has told me that our relationship is unique. One night a few years ago while we were driving away from her house, we were trying to define a "mentoring relationship." She told me, "It's like we're more like friends, but you're an adult friend. I mean, who'd want to hang out with a sixteen-year-old girl?"

So I guess you could say that Chelsea and I are a lot like girlfriends, but with some limitations. Since I'm a generation older than her (in fact I'm several years older than her mom and a few years older than her dad), I do limit how personal I get with her. As she has gotten older, I've shared a bit more—even a few things that aren't going well in my life. However, I think we talk about things that girlfriends might talk about, only with the difference in age adding perspective to our talks. As far as "bigger topics," I've tried to share my wisdom about boys based on my own years of experience with the opposite sex. I've shared my theory with her that boys and men operate on "man time" and don't show interest as soon as a girl might.

Although there were a few boys that she spoke of between sixth grade and eighth grade, she met the first "special" boy at the beginning of her ninth grade year. His name was Andrew and he was going to a private school elsewhere, but lived relatively close to her home. He was a budding rock star, a song writer and a pretty nice guy from what I heard. She'd always get a little dreamy-eyed when talking about him. (He wrote a song for her which definitely earned a place in her heart!)

One evening we sat at a cafe eating ice gelato. Chelsea described what a great kisser he was—because she had been his teacher! (I told her that I remembered a few times when I was much younger, when I was inspired to do the same thing because the guy just didn't have a clue.) That was lots of fun—and I found out she was a whole lot more experienced (and comfortable) than I was at her age.

I remember sitting with her in my SUV one night at a park near her house just talking to each other. We talked about what to do when a boy "wants to go all the way," how to talk about physical boundaries and ask for his partnership in keeping them, and how to keep communication lines open. Ironically, the dating issues she was dealing with as a teenager were not dramatically different than those I was dealing with as a dating adult! I had more choices available to me as an adult, but—truly—she and a boy could make the same choices with less information. I really wanted her to have information to consider and know that she could make her own choices, not just go along with a boy's agenda.

We've also talked about churches, religion and spirituality. We have different backgrounds and beliefs, but we are open to each other's perspectives. We talk about clothes, music, TV and movies and who's "hot" and who's not. To my surprise, Chelsea thinks some male actors in my generation are "hot!" Will wonders never cease?

Chelsea says...

In reference to Paula and Chelsea following different spiritual paths:

Paula's friend: "So you don't think Paula's going to hell?"

Chelsea: "No, I don't. She's got way too many things going for her."

How to Be a Marvelous Mentor

As you start your mentoring journey with your mentee and clarify your role as a mentor, you may be able to use the following nine ways to be "simply mah-velous" as a mentor. These are tried and true qualities and they show up in mentoring studies again and again. If you put these into practice every week, you're off to a great start!

1. Choice and voice in decisions.

The time you offer to a girl once a week might be the only time when she gets to have a choice OR a voice. She might talk nonstop from the beginning to the end of your outing because she knows you care and she's reveling in the joy of an adult being interested in what she has to say. Getting your mentee involved in choosing activities and giving her an equal vote in what you will do together each week shows true partnership and respect. That's a special bond you're forming together. She may be hesitant to share her ideas at first, while she tests your interest in what she has to say and whether it will actually happen. She also may not believe her ideas are actually something you will be willing to participate in with her. Later on, her activity suggestions might become rather expensive (read: Kenny Chesney concert) or just involve a cost you aren't able to afford that week. When these more expensive requests show up, try negotiating—work out an arrangement where the special outing is "earned" or her help with a home project is exchanged for the outing. Another approach is setting limits: "I'm willing to take you and a friend to one concert per year," or, "If we eat out, I have a total of $20.00 for both of us to spend on dinner."

2. Control: She chooses what to talk about and how to talk about it.

In the early days of your relationship, it's extremely important to respect her while she gets to know you and reaches the level of trust that works for her. When trust is earned, talking is made easier—whether you're an adult or a child. Probing and cross-examining her will get you nowhere and could set things back if not derail the bond you're trying to establish. Even though you may be raring to make a difference in this

Chelsea says...

When I tell her something that is important to me, she makes me feel like a princess.

child's life, she may still need a lot of time to warm up to you. On the other hand, she may surprise you and unload more than you expected into your lap in a very short amount of time! Whatever the case, go at her pace and always be a neutral listener. Patience is definitely a virtue in mentoring. From the beginning, always let your mentee know that you are there for her and that she can tell you anything without fear or judgment. Eventually she will take that to heart.

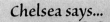

Chelsea says...

Because of our friendship Paula's opinion started to really make a difference.

3. Have fun together!

When you were a child, wasn't it always much more fun when the adults played kickball or went to the movies with you? Suddenly your activity was more important and more exciting! When you participate in activities your mentee considers fun, you really show your interest and your commitment to her. Fun activities are a great way to relax with each other and share time. Later on this fun will lead to the type of indepth conversations between the two of you that is only possible after a relationship is established.

The opportunity to revisit your childhood is part of the mentoring experience. Play Frisbee at the park or watch a "girl power" movie together and talk about it afterwards over ice cream. It will be a completely new experience! Be a good playmate and you'll be surprised what you learn and talk about. Chapter 9 provides many ideas for fun activities that you can enjoy together.

4. Be a positive person and example.

Building her self-esteem and confidence is an important function as a mentor—chapter 7 will focus on this in more detail. No matter how you feel or what kind of day you've had, leave it at home before you go pick up your mentee! Remember, you are part of her support system not a source of negative energy. You don't have to be sappy or fake with her, just be supportive and friendly. Be the dependable oasis that she turns to every week. It's very possible she's already got problems with a number of people in her life (parents, siblings, kids at school or maybe even the juvenile justice system) and your job is to be one of the positive forces in her life. When you do things together, make sure you give her frequent compliments and tell her that you believe in her and her abilities. Specific positive feedback is always the best kind. Be supportive and encouraging—even when she's having a hard time. Your positive words and thoughts are what she needs to help her get through the tough times. If she needs help with schoolwork—and you feel you can help—ask her if she'd like your help. Be direct so she knows that you are interested, but don't be attached to her response. Be aware of how you talk about other people as well as yourself while with your mentee. Set a positive example for her.

5. Help her to solve problems.

After you've gotten to know each other, there will be opportunities to help build your mentee's problem-solving skills by talking through what is going in her life. If it seems appropriate, ask her questions to help her examine the situation more closely: "What do you think you should do?" or, "Why do you think that girl is behaving that way toward you?" Regarding more personal problems ask her, "What is another way of solving this problem?" Keep asking her that question until she figures out a couple of different options from which to choose. Other times if she truly doesn't know which way to go or turn, offer one

Chelsea says...

Once I started trusting Paula, I started putting all of the advice that she offered me into action.

or more solutions that could be useful (ideally refer her to profession-al help). (Note: On my blog www.YouthMentorIdeas.com, extensive information for both "Crisis Resources for Girls and Women" and "Educational Resources for Girls and Women" is available.)

6. Always respect the trust she grants you.

When your mentee chooses to share some personal matters with you, it is critical that you be supportive of her. She is demonstrating her courage by choosing to test your support and friendship by sharing the things that—up until now—have been secrets. Some things she shares might be difficult for you to hear or agree with. Even so, let her know you under-stand her side of the story and that you hear what she is saying. Be neu-tral and supportive and listen carefully. Reassure her that, whatever she shares with you, you are there for her now and in the future. Your com-mitment is real and reliable. If she wants your advice, offer it cautiously

Chelsea says...

Because of some things that happened in my family I tend to lie about things to avoid getting hurt. I lie and manipulate, and do a lot of things to avoid getting in trouble. I've learned through therapy that that's a very common way of dealing with family problems. In my whole history of knowing Paula, I've never lied to her. She's the one person I've never lied to. The reason I've always told her the truth is because I know that she's not going to be disappointed in me. I have always lied to avoid someone looking down on me or to avoid them hurting me. And I know she won't do that to me. I realized this a couple of weeks ago, that I've never lied to her, ever, in my life. I've never even hid anything from her. I mean, sometimes with other people I'll mix up the story so it doesn't look as bad as it really is or so that it looks better. I don't even do that with her. I'm straight. I don't twist things up or try to sound cool because I don't feel that I have to do that to impress her. I already impress her. I mean, she takes time—forty five minutes to an hour—to come all the way over to my house and spend time with me. There's no point in lying to somebody who does something like that.

and keep it focused on finding a solution. Your mentoring relationship is built on trust—never take this for granted. If your mentee shares private information about her family, background or problems, she is respecting you with her trust for you. Be sure to be worthy of that trust that you have both worked so hard to grow. (Note: If health and safety issues arise that affect your mentee or someone in her life—assuming your mentee is a minor—this would normally be an exception. Check with the mentoring organization for guidance.)

7. Have realistic goals and expectations.

Perhaps you will enter your mentoring relationship rather unsure of your abilities or perhaps you'll be all fired up ready to transform your mentee's life. If you have specific performance goals or a hidden agenda, she will recognize it very quickly. It's very probable that many other adults in her life already have their own respective agendas for her or have none at all. Judging who she is or how she behaves with you is a very narrow and unfair view of her. The messages she may be hearing at home or at school could include: "School's not important. I need you to babysit so I can go to work"; "You're a loser just like your father was"; or "Why can't you be more like your sister at school?" It is very important to accept her at face value and focus on developing a trusting friendship. Her overall development as a person is what mentoring should be about in the beginning. More defined goals—perhaps related to school or work—can come later once she knows you are truly there for her. Mentoring is not about you, it's about your mentee. Just because you are interested in playing the piano does not mean your mentee should learn how to play! Meet your mentee at a neutral place; find out what interests she has and figure out how you can support those interests.

8. Relate to her, not to her parents or guardians.

Always keep in mind that you are building a relationship with your mentee, not befriending her parents or guardians at home. In order to build trust, she needs to know that you are an ally, not a person reporting everything to the adults at home. Sometimes this can be a challenge! A delinquent parent may have been told by authorities that their child needs a mentor as a part of her support system. The parent may resent that you're involved and may not be as cooperative as you had hoped. Another parent may want you to get involved in disciplining the child or even buy her clothing. You don't want to cross these family boundaries—that is not your role as a mentor. Relating to her family members sends a message to your mentee that you cannot be trusted. Be cordial but keep a distance from family members—don't get drawn into the family drama, which will undoubtedly "muddy the waters," so to speak. If other members of her family describe what "really happened" (versus your mentee's version) things will start getting cluttered and you will be less able to be a supportive adult friend to her. Be patient with the situation, stay calm and stay connected to your mentee as much as possible. Besides keeping the child as your focus in the relationship, make sure you do not pass judgment on her family in front of her or in front of family members. Listen with empathy and support, not judgment, even if you agree with the girl's negative point of view about her family. Since your goal as a mentor is to build a relationship with your mentee, respecting her version of her world is very important. It shows respect, nonjudgment and a willingness to listen.

9. Building the relationship is your responsibility.

It sure is nice when two people put an equal amount of effort into building a relationship, but these are not realistic expectations in youth mentoring. As a mentor, you need to take the lead in staying in communication with your mentee and organizing activities. You are the adult and you have more skills, ideas and follow-through ability than the girl you are meeting with each week. She may not communicate her thanks or happiness to you in words. It may just be a smile or the fact that she runs up to your car when you arrive each week. I'm reminded of the line from the movie *Field of Dreams*: "Build it and they will come." Build the relationship and she will come around when she's ready. Soliciting your mentee's input about things to do together and doing some minimal research to find out where to do them is part of the arrangement. Older mentees can be asked to do some basic research, but for the most part you are in charge. And most importantly, don't give up on a quiet or noncommunicative girl! She is testing your level of interest and caring and would love to be pleasantly surprised with your tenacity.

Another Perspective on Working with Young People

When I helped facilitate a weekly spiritual support group for teens, my friend Mark established the following guiding principles for the adult mentors working with the teen program. Although the principles are spiritually based, I think they apply in a mentoring program situation as well. Reflecting upon them and putting them into practice has been very helpful in my role as a youth mentor.

Mentor Guiding Principles

1. We accept that Teens are in charge of their own lives and bodies.
2. We listen more than we speak.
3. We are here to serve them not control them.
4. We create a safe container and hold space for free and open communication.
5. We hold the space for new possibilities and new solutions and for transcending old beliefs and paradigms. This includes our own beliefs about right and wrong.
6. We listen without judgment and do not espouse moralities.
7. We teach metaphysical principles of love, power and creativity — not principles of right and wrong.
8. We provide feedback and direct and support the Teens with basic spiritual principles of forgiveness, nonviolence, honor, respect, honesty, integrity, communication (with self, others and Source).

9. We support introspection, self-inquiry and problem solving but we don't fix anyone.
10. We trust that God is active in the community, that everyone in the community has equal access to God and that every problem comes bearing its own solution.
11. We honor Teenagers and understand that this stage of life is living transformation, an appropriate place for exploration, experimentation and self-expression.
12. We may offer our experience, thoughts, and ideas, but we support the Teens in making their own life decisions and honor the decisions they make. (Note: as long as there is no harm to self or others.)

Information provided by: Mark H. Van der Gaag, CorePower Institute, www.corepowercoach.com

Final Thoughts

Have you started picturing yourself talking with your mentee? Going out to dinner with her? Imagining what it's like to reach a level of trust where you and she can talk about almost anything? I hope so! One day in the not-too-distant future you will pine for these quiet days—believe me! In the next chapter I talk about some practical issues that every mentor may encounter as time goes by. Topics such as cultural or religious differences, liability, health and establishing boundaries are covered. I also share how to interact with the other adults in her life as well as recognizing that her home may not be like the home you are used to.

Reflection: Conversation Starters

The list below gives you some "Conversation Starters" that you and your mentee can use and add to. You get to take turns learning about each other—it's the two way street to building trust.

1. My full name is…

2. I think I was given my name because…

3. My birthday is on…

4. If I had a pet, it would be a… (or, I have a pet and it's a…)

5. My favorite color is…

6. My favorite singer is…

7. In my free time, I like to…

8. If I could do any kind of work, I would love to…

9. My favorite book or author is…

10. My best friend is named…

11. If I had magical powers, I would…

12. The TV show or movie that makes me laugh is called…

13. My least favorite thing to do is…

14. I spend a whole bunch of time…

15. I have lived in places called…

16. An adult who really listened to me and helped me was named…

17. School for me is/was….

18. Living at home is…

19. I feel happiest when…

20. My neighbors where I live are…

21. One of my worst days was…

22. One of my best days was…

23. My relationship with my parent or guardian is like this…

24. On the weekend, I look forward to…

25. On the weekend, I don't like to…

26. At home, this is where I fit age-wise…

27. My favorite thing to eat is…

28. The nastiest thing to eat is…

29. The hardest thing for me to do is…

30. The easiest thing for me to do is…

31. My favorite kind of candy is…

32. I'd like to learn how to…

33. I don't like learning to…

34. I know how to…

35. My favorite bedtime snack is…

36. Add your own questions!

CHAPTER FIVE

Practical Issues

Nothing ventured, nothing goofed.
—Dr. Laurence J. Peter—

When Chelsea was in middle school she frequently wanted to go to the school pool for "Open Swim" on the evenings we got together. This seemed to be a popular activity for the kids from her school and she often played in the water with somebody she knew, along with me. One night when we were getting dressed in the locker room she asked me if I could drop off one of her girlfriends on the way back to Chelsea's house because no one at her home could pick her up. As far as I knew, Chelsea was supposed to be the only family member I drove around in my car, but no one from the mentoring program had ever told me about friends! The poor kid only lived a half mile away and I think it was a winter night. Without someone to check with, I decided to carefully give her a ride home.

Rather than try to explain to this friend why I shouldn't really be driving her around, I later explained to Chelsea that it was best if she was my only passenger in the future. At first Chelsea was mortified that she had put me in an awkward position, but I assured her everything worked out fine.

Putting One Foot In Front of the Other

Speaking for myself, I had a lot of fear of the unknown when I was considering getting involved in youth mentoring. Did I have something to contribute? Would I be able to handle the drama associated with a girl from a family I was not part of? Did I have the skills to be a good mentor? Would I get a good match with a girl I could connect to? Could I stay committed for a whole year? Would I worry about her all the time? Would it be more stressful than enjoyable?

You name it, I stressed about it. Sure, a number of things surfaced that I could not have anticipated, but the truth is I kept plugging along. Plenty of wonderful things took place as well—which I could not have anticipated either! So, the reality is there is no crystal ball in youth mentoring. You put one foot in front of the other, learn as you go and be willing to stay connected to your mentee. You've made an agreement, a commitment to this child. She depends on you to be a constant, supportive adult friend in her life. Be the mentor she needs you to be.

Cultural or Religious Differences

You may be matched with a child from a different culture or who practices a different religion—or no religion. This is a great opportunity to learn about her culture or religion. Chelsea and I discovered early on that I went to a nondenominational Unity church and she attended a Southern Baptist church. She asked me plenty of questions to try to understand how my beliefs and church compared to hers. Even though she wasn't familiar with my version of church, she came to accept the differences. I once attended her church with her and her family because she invited me when I was considering finding a new church to attend. We had a respectful, open-mindedness towards each other's choices around religion.

Respect for her, her culture and her religion is very important and will go a long way towards building your relationship and earning the respect of her and her family. An important concept to keep in mind as a mentor is that "different" is not good or bad or right or wrong—it's just different. Be very careful about what kind of meaning you attach to "different" because it will be picked up by your mentee. Admit when you don't understand or know about something she mentions and ask her permission to learn more from her, her parent or guardian. If you disagree with their practices or beliefs, always be respectful and politely tell her, "That is not what I believe, but I respect that you and your family follow that practice." Consider going to the library and doing a little research with or without her so you can share what you have learned when it seems appropriate. Invite her to ask you questions about your own culture or religion whenever she desires.

Liability, Responsibility, Health, Safety and Boundaries

An important task for you to complete before you begin your mentoring role is to clarify your liability, responsibility and risks. You must learn what to do in the event that health and safety issues arise and where you can or should define boundaries. Although mentoring programs are pretty good about telling you what is okay or not okay, it helps to understand why things are done a certain way.

To reduce risk, same-gender matches are pretty much the standard for community-based, one-on-one mentoring relationships. Early in the mentoring application process, you will be carefully screened. The purpose of this screening process is not only to make a great match, but to screen out people who are not appropriate for a mentoring relationship.

Once you begin mentoring, it is very important to stay in communication with your contact at the mentoring organization in case any concerns arise or if you have questions along the way.

Liability, Responsibility and Risks

According to *American Heritage College Dictionary* (Pickett 2007) responsibility is another word for liability. Responsibility is defined as "Something for which one is responsible; a duty, obligation or burden." A mentoring organization must take steps to reduce liability, and whether you are trained in law or not (I am not), you need to understand what liability and responsibility is as it relates to youth mentoring.

At one end of the liability spectrum, liability could mean taking all measures to carefully screen potential mentors so as to avoid pedophiles and/or adults who might harm a child. At the other end of the liability spectrum, a mentoring organization must choose people who are interested in making a real commitment and have qualities and traits that are supportive of building a relationship with a child. Getting a relationship started and having it end abruptly is extremely disappointing to a child. Both ends of the spectrum are very critical to the success of the mentoring relationship and the organization's mission.

As a community-based mentor for example, there is no need for you to be operating at a disadvantage. The organization for which you volunteer should properly orient and/or train you for your mentoring role and should provide continuing support through phone calls, meetings or ongoing training events if appropriate. (Note that the size and budget of a mentoring organization may have an influence on how much training and support you receive.) You need proper information to understand what is involved and when to seek help.

Another example of liability or risk is divulging confidential information about your mentee to individuals outside the program, thus damaging the trust relationship that has been established, not to mention the reputation of the mentoring organization. This is a very serious issue. Mentoring is about a trusting relationship—not necessarily a "given" in the lives of these young people. You always need to assess how your words and actions affect your mentee and the organization for which you volunteer.

Some questions for you to clarify with your mentoring organization about liability and risks are:

1.   Where can I meet with my mentee? What locations are off-limits?
2.   Can I transport her in my vehicle?

3. Can I transport one of her family members or her friends in my vehicle?
4. Is it okay for us to spend time alone, or must we always be with other people?
5. If I'm trying to help her with hygiene, is it okay for her to take a private shower or bath while visiting my home?
6. If she has questions about feminine products or feminine issues, is it okay for me to try to answer them?

Health and Safety Issues

Your mentor role has a limit. You cannot possibly be all things to all people—nor should you be. You are this child's adult friend, supporter, listener and confidante, but that is as far as your responsibility goes. You want her to know that you are always there for her and you are her "partner" and advocate for whatever comes up. However, even if you have training in counseling or social work, it is not your role as a mentor to treat this child as a "client." Check the guidelines for the mentoring organization with whom you are connected regarding health and safety issues and what to do about them.

If your mentee's health and safety are at risk based on something she has told you or something you have observed (e.g., experimenting with drugs or alcohol or perhaps a vision problem), you need to explain to your mentee that as a mentor you are obligated to get her the help she needs from the people that have the best solutions. At a minimum, this will involve telling the mentoring program coordinator or caseworker so the appropriate people get involved. She may be very upset that other people may have to be told, but remind her that you are standing by her side until the problem gets explored and resolved. If you are connected to a mentoring organization, let them initiate the contacts to get professional help and/or to reach out to her family.

If your mentee tells you her concerns about someone else in the family, try to ask questions so you understand what is going on as best you can. You want to clarify if she feels her own health and safety are at risk or if the health and safety of another family member is at risk. Again, explain to her that you treat health and safety issues very seriously, and as a mentor you can help her or her family member get the right kind of help by involving others. Be sure to speak to the program staff within the mentoring organization so they can get the appropriate people involved on behalf of this child.

Some questions for you to clarify with the mentoring organization about health and safety issues are:

1. What is the procedure if my mentee tells me she is being abused or hurt by others?
2. What if she has thoughts of suicide?
3. What if my mentee tells me she has hurt/is hurting someone else?
4. What if my mentee tells me she is hurting herself? (cutting, eating disorders, etc.)
5. What if I suspect my mentee is breaking the law?
6. What if my mentee asks me about birth control or abortion—should I discuss these issues with her?

Boundaries and Behaviors

Depending on the type of mentoring program, your behaviors and the boundaries you have may vary from those set by the program. For example, when I was a mentor in a church Sunday school program, it was very important to always have at least three people in a room rather than one adult and one child alone. This was to protect against liability. In some schools, hugging is not allowed between adults and children or even between children. It is very important to understand the boundaries that need to be set in your role as a mentor, as well as what behaviors are considered appropriate and inappropriate. Just because you wouldn't give something a second thought at home does not mean the same rules apply as a mentor.

Also be aware that once you get connected to your mentee's family, you might be looked upon as an "extra adult" that can be called upon to do other things for your mentee and/or the family. Inviting you to attend her school play is completely fine. Asking you to babysit your mentee and her siblings is quite another thing. Make sure you run unusual requests past the program staff within your mentoring organization.

Some questions for you to clarify with the mentoring organization about boundaries and behaviors are:

1. Can I give her a hug?
2. Can she stay overnight at my home on occasion?
3. Can I take her to someone else's home who is a friend or family member?
4. Can we exchange phone numbers?
5. Can we exchange e-mails, text messages or instant messages on the computer? Can I "friend" her on Facebook?
6. What level of contact is appropriate with my mentee's family?
7. Can I invite a member of my family along for an outing with my mentee?
8. What if her family member asks me to run an errand during my time with my mentee?
9. What if I'm asked to pick up my mentee from school, the doctor, or other places because the parent/guardian is unavailable?
10. What if I'm asked to babysit my mentee and/or her younger siblings by a parent/guardian?
11. On occasion, can I spend time with my mentee in the company of one of my friends who has a child her age?
12. If I have professional skills that may be helpful, should I tell her or her family or offer my skills if I think they would be helpful?
13. Is it okay to give or receive gifts?
14. Is it okay to talk about my family/life/job/significant other with my mentee?
15. If I have a particular political/religious/lifestyle belief or a strong opinion about certain things, can I share them with my mentee?

The Adults in Her Life: How to Relate to Them

Adults in Her Family

As I've already mentioned, it's important to maintain a cordial relationship with the adults in your mentee's family, but I don't advocate a close relationship or friendship with them. Your priority is your relationship with your mentee and building trust with her. Getting close to another family member takes away from your relationship with her, and may affect the level of trust between the two of you.

You will want to have the phone numbers of her parents and/or guardians so you can clarify logistics and schedules as required. Whenever I picked up Chelsea, I always greeted the family members present and participated in some basic chit-chat about superficial topics. Chelsea typically had an expectant "Can we go now?" look on her face, so we generally left quickly after I arrived. Although there have been occasions when I was contacted by Chelsea's dad about problems that had come up with her, for the most part he and I just wave hello or goodbye. At the beginning, I made it a point to keep him well informed about what we had planned, what movie we were going to see, or schedule changes that he should be aware of. Later on, when my weekly appearance was more routine and I had established a level of trust with him, the extra efforts were not needed as much.

You May Be Seen as a Threat by Other Adults at Her Home

Sometimes, a parent or guardian might feel threatened by your involvement in his or her child's life. At first, a mentor seemed like the right choice. Later, this person might see you gaining the child's trust and acceptance and feel insecure about his or her own parenting skills. Other adults may feel you are judging them or trying to turn the child against them, which may be completely untrue.

Chelsea's own dad recently admitted that at first he was torn about whether seeking out a mentor for her was a good idea. "I have had some opportunities to get to know Paula over the years. It was really difficult at first...I felt like I was somehow shirking my responsibilities by letting another person care for and nurture Chelsea. I have grown over the years to appreciate everything that Chelsea and Paula have put into their relationship and recognize how their relationship has complemented my own parenting as well. This truly is a mentoring success story!"

You may find yourself trying to reach a parent to confirm your weekly get-together with your mentee, and she or he does not return your phone calls or doesn't have the child at home when you arrive to pick her up. Don't take this personally! Be calm, keep showing up and try to keep communication going between you and the adults at the home. It is important to be polite and respectful with the child's parent or guardian, especially when the child is also present. Even in a dysfunctional family situation, a child still has the capacity to love the adults at home. If she wants to talk about them to you, remember to stay neutral and, if she is receptive, help her sort out her feelings. You can acknowledge what she's sharing with you by asking, "How does that make you feel?" or saying something like, "You must be very sad," or, "It sounds very tough at home right now." Again, as her mentor, you are not in a position to be critical about her family members or home environment in front of her or with people that are not connected to the mentoring program.

The Other Adults in Her Life

This is an idea I became aware of only recently (thank you Christine Steele!) and I wish I would have known about it much earlier in my mentoring experience. You may have occasion to meet some of the other adults in your mentee's life, such as relatives, teachers, school counselor or minister, through different family, school or church gatherings. Even if you don't have such occasions, it may be a good idea to track down these people and introduce yourself. (Check with your mentoring organization to verify this is okay and whether you should inform the family and/or your mentee of your plans.)

Reaching out to these adults is a great opportunity to gather the names and contact information of your mentee's support system—people that are genuinely interested in and concerned about your mentee. Make sure you let them know who you are, what your mentoring role entails, what organization you represent (if applicable) and that you see your mentee on a regular basis. Although I met a few of Chelsea's relatives, it would have been even better to meet with the school staff that knew her in addition to her church minister. For example, even though Chelsea rarely asked for my help with schoolwork, I knew she had trouble with certain subjects and especially how they were being taught given her learning disability. I think I could have offered more help had I understood her needs better through the eyes of her teachers or school counselor.

The Place She Calls Home

It's possible that your mentee lives in a lower economic neighborhood and you might feel a little uncomfortable or unsafe driving into that community, especially if it is new to you. If you have concerns, share them with the program staff of your mentoring organization. They may have safety tips or suggestions for you to use when picking her up and dropping her off. Remember, you are not spending time with her in her neighborhood, but are taking her someplace else for a few hours.

No matter how you feel about this neighborhood, your mentee considers it home. Be careful what you say or how you refer to the neighborhood (or her neighbors) while you are with her. Show respect for her by showing respect for her neighborhood.

Take normal precautions to secure your car and possessions; don't leave your cell phone, purse or valuables in plain view when you leave the car to go up to her door. Close the windows and lock your doors every time. Park in a well-lit area if at all possible. Greet the neighbors when you see them and treat them respectfully. You would be surprised how far respectful treatment goes and how much it could protect your vehicle and your possessions in your absence.

Final Thoughts

Creating a new mentoring relationship with a child requires learning about each other, building trust and interacting with people that are related to her. It is a good idea to avoid making assumptions about what you would consider standard procedures and behaviors, whether it is with your mentee or her family members. You may find she comes from a very different home and has a different lifestyle than your own. It's not wrong or bad—it's just different. You are not there to judge your mentee's home life or the adults who live there; you are simply there for her.

Building self-confidence as a mentor will take some time. You aren't expected to know all the tricks and tools of the trade right away! The next chapter will provide you with some mentoring tools and advice on how to become a great mentor.

Reflection: Practical Issues

After you meet your mentee and her family, you will undoubtedly discover other things that you're not quite sure how to address. Talking to your mentee or her family members might shed some light. Talking to your contact at the mentoring program might help too. Another idea is to ask the mentoring program to connect you with another experienced mentor. No worries! You have lots of help.

Use the table on the following page to write down some other practical issues that you thought of while reading this chapter.

	Practical Issues That Surfaced
1	
2	
3	
4	
5	
6	
7	
8	
9	
10	

CHAPTER SIX

Building Confidence
in Your Mentoring Abilities

We ourselves feel that what we are doing is just a drop in the ocean.
But the ocean would be less because of that missing drop.
—Mother Theresa—

W hen Chelsea was in the eighth grade, I was a volunteer facilitator at the Thursday evening "Teen Peace Circle" for high school students at my church, Renaissance Unity. The Peace Circle was a support group of sorts where like-minded people came together in a spiritual community and welcomed each other, prayed together, shared what was going on in their lives and asked for feedback. My friend Mark and I facilitated the Teen Peace Circle. Between eight and twenty high school students showed up on any given Thursday.

I truly loved the program because the assumption was that teens are in charge of their lives and bodies. Mark used to say, "I don't see them as 'kids.' They can make the same adult choices as you or me, but they have *less experience*." Our role as Circle facilitators was to listen more than speak, to serve them more than control them, and to create a safe container for free and open communication. We listened without judgment and did not espouse moralities.

We offered guidance or our own experiences if our teens requested feedback, and we honored their decisions as long as there was no harm to self or others. Mark and I worked very well together and we learned a lot from the teens and about ourselves in the process. I wanted Chelsea to experience the love, support and the wonderful atmosphere that our group created every Thursday night.

When we went to the Circle for the first time, it was a summer night and the group met out on the lawn of the church. Chelsea was asked to introduce herself to the group and to participate in the "weaving in" exercise, which involved one person saying to the next person on the left: "We bow before the spirit within and receive into our hearts our beloved sister Chelsea." The group then went into Silence and with eyes closed shared with the group a short description of what they saw for their lives or for the world.

Everyone was then invited to share what was going on in their lives and—as I expected—Chelsea raised her hand. She has always felt comfortable sharing herself with people and is very warm and authentic when she does so. She ended up fitting right in with the group not only with what she shared but also with the feedback she offered to other teens during the evening. I introduced her to a few girls and she stayed in touch with them after that evening.

This was an amazing experience for me too. I had the opportunity to bring together a girl I cared for deeply and a group of people that meant so much to me, so that they could enjoy and experience each other in our spiritual community. It was awesome! I remember Mark told me several times, "I love her energy!" That was especially memorable, because I loved her energy too! Chelsea valued meeting this new group of people that were her age, in a different church than her own, with a different approach to spirituality. She understood that when it comes to spiritual paths, different does not have to be wrong.

I took Chelsea to at least two other Peace Circles, including the last meeting of the group when Mark chose to move on to another type of work. The final Circle—held off-site—was an emotional night because it was the end of an era for the group. It was a night of gratitude for our special spiritual community, full of goodbyes since many of the teens were leaving for college and full of sadness that we wouldn't be gathering again.

After the Circle ended and we said goodbye to everyone, I drove Chelsea to her girlfriend's house where she was going to spend the night. I got out of the car to give her a hug goodbye—not something I did very much in our relationship, but that night seemed extra special. After our hug she said, "I love you Paula!" I was momentarily stunned and I realized I felt the same way! "I love you too Chelsea—I really do!" Up until that night, I knew I cared for Chelsea very much, but it took her to help me realize and articulate that I truly loved her. We hugged again, she thanked me for bringing her to the Circle and we both walked away changed people.

Chelsea says...

After I learned to trust Paula I told her that I loved her. It took me a good three years to be able to say that. I mean, usually, you would think saying "I love you" is nothing. Usually teens say "I love you" a lot, but this is a different friendship and relationship. Pretty much ever since I said "I love you" to Paula, I've taken "I love you" as a very delicate three words. *Very precious.* It just shows that "I love you" is something that you don't take for granted.

Dealing With Your Insecurities

Even though you may not own a Wonder Woman costume, you can still be a wonderful mentor. Your mentee wants a warm, supportive woman in her life, not a larger-than-life super hero. You can handle what you are presented with; just take things one step at a time and you'll be fine. You might be matched with a young person from a different culture, country and/or very different socioeconomic background than your own. You might find yourself having self-confidence issues, and thinking, "Can I handle this?" But, just for a moment think from a different perspective: How do you suppose the child feels?

She has less world experience and fewer resources and people skills than you, and undoubtedly has had very few positive encounters with adults. Yet here you are, a stranger being nice to her for reasons she does not completely understand. When you see things from her perspective, who do you suppose needs more support in this relationship? She does! Let me repeat: Your job is to build the relationship!

Do you think you will have to answer every question and solve every problem your mentee presents to you? No! In my early mentor days, I sometimes caught myself thinking that I must be a "Super Problem Solver." I panicked when I realized I not only wasn't a super hero, but that I might encounter brand new situations and challenges involving a child, where I had little or no experience. That was a sobering realization! All I had to bring to the mentoring "front" was little old me, Paula Dirkes, New Mentor. I had worked with kids in group settings—classrooms, swim lessons, day camp—but rarely one on one. I was the adult in this relationship though, and it was my responsibility to build the relationship. So, I kept moving forward, one step at a time. I was going to make this work!

Overcoming your insecurities about mentoring a child is important for your own self-esteem. However, to instill self-worth in another human being you need to find that inner strength you know you have. If you say, "I don't think I have much to offer," you're not really giving yourself a chance to find out, are you? As the quote from Mother Theresa indicates at the beginning of this chapter, how can you possibly undervalue your personal "drop in the ocean" in this child's life? You could be the "drop" that turns things around for her.

We all go through a period in our lives when we feel insecure, unsure, and have issues of self-doubt that keep us from participating in life's events. The one aspect of mentoring that is mentioned over and over again in training manuals is that "this is not about you; this is about the mentee." You are there for her, and that is most important.

Imagine a child who comes from either a broken home or lives in a household where verbal and physical abuse is the norm, rather than the exception. Imagine a child who has come to this country for a good education, only to find that he or she is bullied because of race or religion. Imagine a child in elementary school who comes home to an empty house because his or her single mom works three shifts in order to meet the bills. Imagine a teenage girl being influenced by the media to grow up too fast and to get sexually active way too soon. Imagine....

If you can put aside your own insecurities and look at the broader picture, you may find that your world is pretty good compared to that of the above-mentioned children. It may be hard to realize, but most of these children need a trustworthy adult friend—someone who will be there for them consistently, who will listen to them without judging them, who will take them places they've never been or just hang out and talk.

To say you don't think you have much to offer is a cop-out! I know those are strong words, but I fervently believe them. You have your life experience at the very minimum. It doesn't matter if you've never traveled or what type of work you do, nor does it matter what ethnicity or religion you ascribe to. What matters is that you can make a difference in a child's life because you are who you are, with all your faults and foibles.

Chelsea says...

Because of Paula I can never stop saying this, I have learned respect for myself. I have so much more respect for myself since we've been friends.

Confidence "Tools"

The truth is, I didn't (and still don't) always know the answer, but my confidence in the "not knowing" (in any part of my life) always improves with time. I always tried to be authentic with Chelsea; if I didn't know the answer I told her so. Sometimes I said, "Let's figure that out together," and we visited the library or went online or did some brainstorming together. When Chelsea was sharing a problem in her life, I always reminded myself that listening was the most powerful "tool" I possessed as a mentor, and I could always offer it to her.

You can be of enormous help to this brave girl by being as patient as possible. Let her know that if she has questions about you, that you would love her to ask them so she can get to know you. Ask her if it's okay for you to ask a few questions about her so you can get to know her too. Let her know you will always ask permission first—and be sure to do just that! Let her know that she is in control and that you respect her wishes. Steer away from personal questions until you have achieved a mutual level of comfort. At the beginning (and if applicable), you might ask about her country or culture or where she grew up. You may find that even though you are from different backgrounds, there is a middle ground where you can both build a strong relationship.

As the relationship continues to blossom, so will your confidence and the confidence of your mentee. It is important to establish that you will really listen to and respect what she has to say. This could be a rare commodity in her life. It is very easy to plan activities in order to avoid talking, but an important purpose of mentoring is to befriend the mentee so that she will be able to talk about whatever is on her mind at any given time. Mutual trust and respect will enhance the relationship.

The more confidence you show, the more the mentee will embrace you as a role model, confidante and friend. Together you can make a difference in each other's lives.

You Have Gifts and Abilities to Share

The first step in building your confidence as a mentor is to examine the gifts that you will inevitably bring to the relationship. I am sure you have plenty of gifts and abilities to share! Here are some that come to mind:

- Life experience
- Commitment to showing up
- Active listening
- Friendship
- Support
- Encouragement
- Trust/trustworthiness

- Undivided attention
- Sharing your life
- Sharing your family
- Sharing your friends
- Sharing your stories
- Skills
- Transportation in your vehicle
- Hugs
- Understanding
- Laughter
- Sense of humor
- Unique personality
- Respect
- Knowledge

The list could go on. Does this make sense? Your presence and attention are what a child needs. Neither requires special training, just a willingness to get involved and grow together over time.

Chelsea says...

Because Paula focuses on the positive she always brought me up too. I remind myself, "Paula doesn't say negative things to herself, so I'm not going to either." If it weren't for her, I would be negative about everything.

A lot of the impact you will have on your mentee (notice the word "will" because I believe it is a certainty) may not be recognized until much later. If you are looking for acknowledgement, you may or may not get it from her or her family. But believe what I am telling you based on my ten years of mentoring—the light you bring into her life shines brightly in her heart and is building her self-esteem and trust every day. You are making a difference! Whether she is mad or glad, pouty or chatty, quiet or crying, you are slowly building a solid relationship. One day, out of the blue you will know that you have earned her trust. And it will all be worth the trip!

"Who the Heck Am I???"

If you think I'm reading your mind—you're wrong! I'm just remembering the little voice in my head talking up a storm back in my pre-mentoring days. In case I <u>was</u> reading your mind, consider yourself "normal." I don't think any of us grow up thinking, "Someday, I will be a spectacular resource and mentor to a young girl!"

Let me try to read your mind some more and really get your thoughts out on the table, okay?

"Why would a girl and her parents want to trust me? I'm a stranger!"

In the first place, if you are in a mentoring program, the family knows you have been well-screened to be a mentor. Being a mentor with a program involves very specific guidelines and boundaries. Yes, the news is out there about the unfortunate examples of how some adults have taken advantage of children. Everyone involved needs to build a level of trust; this takes time and patience. Just because you've decided to change the world through mentoring, does not make you immediately trustworthy in a girl's eyes or her family's eyes. Start slow and be consistent. New relationships develop with time. Be sure to stay in touch with staff members who have lots of experience in this area.

"What if she doesn't talk—I'll feel so uncomfortable!"

One day you'll ask yourself, "Does she ever take a breath?" But at the beginning, put yourself in her shoes. Were you comfortable talking to an adult "stranger" when you were her age? Did adults really care what you had to say or about the thoughts you wanted to share? Maybe not, maybe so. Your task as a mentor is to make it clear over time that you're available and interested in listening to her if and when she's ready to share. While she is warming up to you, share anecdotes with her and ask open-ended questions that require her to share a little more. Talk about the music on her favorite radio station: "Who's your favorite female singer? Why?" If she's an *American Idol* fan ask her, "Why do you think [insert most recent winner's name] won *American Idol*?" Talk about "safe" topics and they will eventually lead to topics closer to her heart.

"I'm so much older than her" and/or "I'm not very 'cool'—how can we relate?"

Nobody said you should be able to relate on all levels. She doesn't expect you to be cool either. Chances are she has no interest in being "just like you" or vice versa. You are individuals brought together to connect from your respective places. She is just as nervous as you—perhaps more so if her adult role models have not been the best thus far. Your world view is larger than hers; she may want to hear what you have to say because you are older and "wiser" on certain topics. This is an opportunity for both of you to learn about and respect each other's differences and to be authentic with each other. (You will be practicing authenticity sooner than she will.) That is one of the reasons why a mentoring relationship is so special. You can teach each other! What about that iPod you bought but don't know how to use—I bet your mentee knows what to do! If you have a gift for studying techniques,

Chelsea says...

Whether you realize it or not, you're mentoring everybody every day. Some little girl or some little boy that sees you with a smile on your face, they'll remember that. You don't have to be "cool," you don't have to have "cool" clothes, you don't have to listen to "cool" music. I don't even know what "cool" means. "Cool" meant something when I was younger, but cool is who you are as a person. If you can mentor somebody during the day, or just one time a week, that's what matters most.

cooking simple hot meals or doing research on the Internet, you can share these gifts with your mentee. Look for the common ground to start, and branch out from there.

"What if a heavy topic comes up and I don't know what to do?"

"Heavy topics" can be part of anybody's life, including your mentee's. Your role as a mentor is NOT to fix, repair or take over the problems of the child. You are there as an adult friend who can listen, help to work through things and be a positive role model. It is important to maintain the confidence of your mentee, but where their health and safety is concerned you need to follow mentoring guidelines and/or warn them that those are exceptions and you need to inform the appropriate people. Chapter 5 focused on practical issues like these. There is also plenty of great information on my blog—www.YouthMentorIdeas.com—that covers both crisis and educational resources for both mentors and mentees.

"What if I say or do something wrong? I'm afraid of making a mistake."

Mentors are people too—and no one can be a perfect role model at all times. Whether a swear word (or two) comes out of your mouth while driving with her on a congested street, or you inadvertently say something that is embarrassing or even hurtful to her, you always have the opportunity to apologize to her and admit you were wrong. What an amazing example you are setting by doing so! How many other adults in her life do you suppose make this a practice? Not too many I would guess. You show your respect for her by showing her accountability for your own actions. This is a quality that she can learn and use in her own life.

"What if we don't seem to get along?"

A mentoring match grows with time and attention. Your job as a mentor is to follow through on your commitment to this child—you are the adult in this match. Just a reminder: this child undoubtedly has lots of experience with one or more adults who constantly remind her she's not worthy/important/good/smart enough. Then again, she may be used to receiving very little feedback from adults or being completely ignored. The reality is she may not trust adults right now, or she may want to trust an adult, but she is afraid to let herself be vulnerable and let down again. Being guarded, sullen, quiet, rude or unappreciative may be part of how she protects herself. She is testing whether you will stick around! It takes baby steps and patience to build a trusting relationship.

What can you do? Always try to model the good behavior you would like her to learn. Praise her whenever possible. Give her realistic choices and follow through with her choice. Keep showing up, share your time and keep listening. Be the adult who is worthy of her trust. Things will improve after she realizes you are not going away. Always share any of your concerns with the program coordinator.

"How will I fill ALL that time together?"

See chapter 9 for lots of ideas!

Final Thoughts

I am sure you are feeling more confident about your gifts and abilities as a mentor. Remember, I was in your shoes back in 2000! I thought your thoughts. I had every rationale and every excuse. I had a full life, or so I thought. My reasons were not the noblest when I signed up (e.g., guilt), but I did it anyway. I'm so pleased with the outcome of my relationship with Chelsea and that we've written this book together! You just never know what's in store for you and your mentee.

Now that you are on your way to becoming a confident mentor, let's look at building your mentee's self-confidence. Chapter 7 provides some strategies for reinforcing your mentee's self-esteem and self-confidence.

Reflection: Your Abilities

I don't know about you, but I sometimes have a hard time recognizing my own "wonderfulness!" Maybe it's my Catholic upbringing or adults telling me as a child "not to brag." For me, the easier approach to recognizing my own skills and abilities is to view myself through other people's eyes. The table on the following page helps you view yourself through other people's eyes and assists you in identifying in yourself traits or abilities that may be very useful as a mentor. It's a "mentoring memory jogger" just for you.

Your Mentoring Memory Jogger	
What qualities do your friends say you have? (These may come in handy with your mentee!)	The qualities my friends say I have are:
What does your family appreciate about you? (Would these assist you with your mentee?)	My family appreciates these things about me:
What abilities do your coworkers rely on from you? (Would these be helpful in your mentoring role?)	My coworkers rely on these abilities from me:
What qualities do you appreciate in a good friend? (You can offer some of the same qualities to your mentee too.)	My good friends have these qualities:
When you think of the formal/informal mentors in your life while growing up, what qualities made them special? (Continue the legacy!)	The qualities of the mentors of my life are:
What are your favorite hobbies and/or free time activities? (Maybe there is some common ground or things to learn from each other!)	My favorite hobbies/free time activities are:
What skills and/or abilities could you share with a child? (Check to make sure she's interested first, and don't forget to ask her to teach you too!)	My skills and abilities include:
Think of children who are related to you, or who you babysat. What makes those relationships special? Why are you their "favorite?" What efforts do you make to keep the relationships special? (A mentoring relationship can be another place to build something special too!)	How would the young people in my life describe why I'm their "favorite?"

Nice start! But are you being a little modest? (You can add more later!)
You're going to realize many more attributes that you bring to mentoring
once you get going—guaranteed.

CHAPTER SEVEN

Building Your Mentee's Confidence

Children are likely to live up to what you believe of them.
—Lady Bird Johnson—

A s I've mentioned earlier, listening is a quality well worth developing as a mentor. While I learned how important it is to listen, I also learned that some of the things that Chelsea needed to tell me wouldn't be easy to hear.

When I met Chelsea, she was eleven-and-a-half years old and in fifth grade. She had been held back a year in fourth grade due to some difficulties with school, learning and the effects of her parents' divorce. In addition to being a year older than her ten-year-old classmates at her elementary school, her body had matured early and she was taller and more physically developed.

My memories of being different in ANY way as a child are not pleasant. Chelsea was in the thick of it, and when I picked her up during those first weeks for our get-togethers, she was often upset about kids picking on her or calling her names. There was one particular bully that made it his daily mission to make her miserable. Having been picked on myself—even into my high school years—for looking like a boy, being short and being a "brain," I could relate to her anguish completely.

Although it took her quite a while, Chelsea eventually told me that she was often called a "slut." "Slut???!!!" I was incredulous. "She's in grade school! Do they even know what that word means??" A large part of me wanted to go grab a few of these kids and shake them like rag dolls! But...I was a mentor—I needed to be calm and a good listener. I found myself sounding like my mother used to: "Try to ignore them Chelsea. They'll lose interest in picking on you. Just be the great person that you are!" I assured her they would eventually back off and recognize how nice she really was. At the same time, I recalled that these platitudes never seemed to work when I was young. Chelsea continued to report on the bullying and I continued listening and supporting her. I couldn't be there with her, but I certainly could be there for her.

Looking back, Chelsea said something that reminds me it's true that the more things change, the more they remain the same. At the time, she was being bullied because she had some facial hair that a few boys decided was worthy of their daily harassment. The poor girl did all sorts of things—plucking, burning chemicals—to make herself feel better about it. Upon reflection, Chelsea now says, "A lot of boys made fun of me then, and now I come to find out that all those guys that were being mean to me, liked me!"

Probably we all have similar stories to that of Chelsea's. Even though I didn't feel particularly effective in making her problem go away, Chelsea has assured me that my listening ear was extremely helpful and meaningful to her, while she developed her self-confidence.

Building Her Confidence in Herself

Being a supportive mentor means not only showing up and actively listening to your mentee, but also cheering her on and building her self-esteem and confidence through your interaction with her. I would venture to say these are all skills you practice on a regular basis with many people in your life—family, friends, neighbors or even co-workers. In my experience with Chelsea, I have found the following strategies helped her to build her self-confidence over time. I didn't know of these strategies when we first started meeting, I assure you. I gathered them over time and stored them in my "mentoring toolbox." I hope they are helpful to you now.

Give Her Choices

Even though I spent—and still spend—the majority of my time together with Chelsea engaged in listening to her talk, I'm not totally silent. One thing I feel comfortable talking about with Chelsea, and did from the first, was her ability to choose. I consistently tried to remind her, "You always have choices Chelsea. You can make a new choice every minute, hour or day if you like." As the visits went by, sometimes I would remind her of another choice that she had made previously or that we talked about before so she could consider using that choice again in a similar situation.

When she came to me about being bullied in elementary school, I did my best to give her more than just the usual platitudes to hang on to. Every time she brought up the latest bullying episode, I gently reminded Chelsea that what someone else said about her was just one opinion; it wasn't the only choice. I reminded her that she was a great person to me, to her brothers and sister, to her dad, to her friends and anyone else that came to mind and that the bully probably wasn't feeling good about him or herself and was taking it out on Chelsea. Whenever it seemed appropriate, I'd encourage Chelsea to exercise her choice to overlook what the bully

Chelsea says...

I made a lot of poor choices growing up and Paula took an hour out of her week to make my life what it is now. Even if we don't get together, or if we just talk for fifteen minutes during the week, when I make a decision, (she may not realize this), every time I make a decision that is important I think about what my parents would say and what Paula would say.

was saying to her and remove herself from the situation as quickly as possible so she didn't have to cope with more abuse. I reminded her that what the bully wanted was attention, and participating in a debate or fighting back was not the way to solve the problem.

Ask Her: What Do You Think?

When Chelsea was in middle school, I also tried to help her sort through the bully's behavior or the "mean girl's" behavior by asking her, "What do you think?" We brainstormed about what might be behind that behavior. Was this a person that felt good about himself or not? Why did she think a person would behave that way—was it because he or she really was mean or was it just to get attention? Did the person have lots of friends of their own or not? I tried to get her to think beyond the superficial comments and behavior and think about why the bullying was occurring.

In these situations—in every situation—I encouraged Chelsea to think things through and make decisions and choices for herself, rather than let other people and circumstances dictate who she was or how she should feel about herself. I figured the more choices she had to consider, the more empowered she could be! After all, I'm only with her once a week and even her dad can't and won't be with her every minute of the day. Besides, it's his job—not mine—to pass on his values to her. My job is to encourage Chelsea to use those values, and the ones she's developing as she matures, to make decisions she can be proud of later. Of course, this also means I've bitten my tongue, sometimes literally, on more than one occasion....

Give Her Responsibilities

Money Transactions

Another way I tried to build Chelsea's self-confidence was by giving her different responsibilities when we were together or between our get-togethers. For example, if we were at a restaurant I would get her involved in figuring out the tip amount for our waitress. Even though math was not her specialty, I tried to help her apply it in a real world setting every once in a while. If I paid for our food bill with cash, I handed the bill and money to Chelsea and asked her to pay our bill, deliver a certain amount to the table as a tip for our waitress and give me the change if any. Later, when Chelsea was in high school, I took some money management information I had learned at a training program, tweaked it and created a money management system that she could use with the babysitting money she was earning. I don't know for a fact that she put it into use, but it's available if she wants to start.

Calendars and Planning

Early on, Chelsea's dad put her in charge of coordinating her outings with me. He did not want to be the "middle man," so it was up to her to keep us updated if things changed. I got her a calendar and asked her to write things down so she wouldn't double book our nights together, especially if we had to change or cancel our evening for some reason. For a while, I also called Chelsea's dad to make sure he knew of changes that occurred, but for the most part she and I had figured out a pretty good planning system.

Chelsea also knew she could call me at home if something came up. On a few occasions we got our wires crossed (e.g., I'm in her driveway and nobody's at home), so I found myself asking her, "Does your dad (or grandmother) know we're switching to Tuesday starting next week?" I had to learn to trust that the arrangements we agreed upon actually made it to her calendar and/or were discussed with her dad or grandmother before we saw each other the following week. I can only imagine what it's like to be a parent with multiple kids and numerous activities and appointments to keep track of!

Shopping and Errands

After I got past my early paranoia that she would run away or be kidnapped when I wasn't looking, I gave Chelsea certain items to track down when we were at the grocery store, just to make the trip go a little faster. For example, if we were at Office Depot, while I was searching for the right printer cartridges in one area of the store, I'd send Chelsea with some cash to get some copies run for me at the photocopy center on the other side of the store.

Think of Your Own Ideas

Any type of life skill or task that you can teach and assign to her shows that you are confident in her and that you trust her to complete it. When we lived closer during the first few years, we did a little baking and some cooking together. When we were driving to a new location, I got her involved in reading a map and playing "navigator." Be flexible, give up your need to control everything and you will be pleased that you have a wonderful partner in your mentee!

Chelsea says...

She's always pushed me to follow my dreams, to just go with something if I like it, to have fun and still be serious about other things.

Let Her Be a Mentor Too

Chelsea hasn't just grown into a young woman I'm proud to introduce to my family; she has grown into someone who has taught me a few things as well. I think a natural outgrowth of spending time with preteens and teenagers is their fascination and current knowledge of music, movies, fashion, technology and the Internet—just to name a few interests. Chelsea is my personal guide to the world of teenagers and I like it!

Music Expertise

Chelsea is definitely the pop culture resource in our relationship. (I admit that when she was about twelve, I listened to the same track from the band O-Town one hundred times too many, but I survived and she got older and her music taste became more diverse.) Chelsea has her "own" car radio buttons reserved in my car and she is constantly quizzing me on which artist is singing at any given moment—I fail most of the time! But I've learned her favorite artists, so I choose from the "usual suspects" and I sometimes get it right. She'll look at me with a surprised facial expression and say, "Im-PRESS-ive Paula!" and hold up her hand for a high five whether I'm driving or not. She makes me laugh every time. I now can identify Kenny Chesney (most of the time), Gretchen Wilson (sometimes) and Usher now and then. Of course I quiz her right back with 70s and 80s artists, and more times than not, she'll know who they are—that amazes me!

The bonus moment is when a song comes on the radio and we both start singing the lyrics. I really freak her out when I start singing the lyrics of what she considers a current song, when in fact it's a remake of an old song. At any rate, she covers many more decades of music than I can—I'm sort of stuck in the 70s somewhere. I remember when I first met her she promptly announced, "I listen to music 24-7!" Im-PRESS-ive Chelsea!

Technology and Teenagers

Technology is not exactly Chelsea's expertise (nor mine), but she has enough teenager knowledge to be dangerous—in a good way. When she got an iPod last year she wowed me by bringing it into my car with some sort of adaptor that allowed her to play her iPod music through my car radio! "How cool is that?" I exclaimed. I had no clue that such a gizmo was available, but thanks to Chelsea, I became enlightened. As a result I bought an MP3 player so I could listen to audio files in my car for an Internet Marketing course I am pursuing. I couldn't figure out how to easily adjust the volume and was feeling kind of "old" and very frustrated. I shared my problem with Chelsea in hopes that she could help me out. She grabbed it and quickly showed me how to use the illuminated wheel on the front of the device—duh!

Just Who is the Mentee Here?

Chelsea and I both have siblings, and sometimes we talk about our challenges with them especially when one of our siblings decides they know how to live our lives better than we do. When Chelsea was about sixteen, one of my sisters came to visit me and accompanied us on our weekly outing for a quick lunch and a movie. During this outing, my sister was being her sometimes opinionated self. I generally get quiet when one of my sisters starts telling me how she thinks I should run my life. Perhaps it's because I am the youngest of my siblings. Besides the sisterly dynamic, I didn't want to argue with her in front of Chelsea.

The next week I told Chelsea, "My sister enjoyed meeting you."

Chelsea said, "Yeah—she was nice...."

Silence. It appeared she had more to say, but wasn't sure if she should. So I casually asked, "Is there something else you wanted to say?"

Chelsea responded immediately. "She needs to learn that thing you always say: Fire the Judge!" I happened to have a Post-it note with the words "Fire the Judge" on my car's dashboard as a reminder to me not to judge myself so harshly. I had explained why it was there to Chelsea the first week that she saw it, and now she pointed at my dashboard Post-it note meaningfully. Then she went on to say, "She acted like she didn't even know you—like I know you! She wasn't very nice to you. I wanted to say something, but I knew I should respect an adult and keep my mouth shut. But if she ever comes to visit again, I'm going to speak up!"

Chills ran through me! I was quite amazed that Chelsea picked up on the dynamic between my sister and me. I thought about what Chelsea said, and told her that she was extremely insightful and thanked her for her support of me—it was kind of a neat surprise! Nothing slips by Chelsea. This mentoring stuff is not all one-sided; Chelsea shares her insights when I need to hear them.

Chelsea says...

I'm growing and I'm maturing in so many ways, just from every relationship that I'm in, whether it be a boyfriend at one time, or a friendship. I learned from our relationship what a real true friendship looks like and what real intimate friendships and love are.

Chelsea's Evolving Self-Confidence

As I look back over our ten years together, it's easy to identify the times when Chelsea's self-confidence took a leap forward, even though at the moment, it may not have been as apparent. Chelsea sometimes has a habit of telling me about a learning or insight she got from our time together well after the time has passed! Whether she shared it with me in the moment—or ever—is not so important. The fact that she grew is the important part. I'm really pleased that I could be part of it and honored that she attributes some of the support to me. I share these personal stories with you to give you some examples of experiences you may encounter and some glimpses of the growth and change you can look forward too.

The World of Boys

As long as I've known Chelsea, she has always craved having a "best friend," someone she could trust to be with her through "thick and thin." Her desire for close connections certainly predates meeting me.

Chelsea's dad once told me that when she was in kindergarten, she would stand in the middle of the playground and cry her eyes out if none of the children wanted to play with her. It was all very personal to her, and it stayed that way during our early years as mentor and mentee. All too frequently during those years, she would announce her new "best friend" to me, who would soon be replaced by another.

Boys have been an ongoing theme in Chelsea's life almost since I met her. She seemed to have some difficulty connecting with girls her age and (I think) turned to boys instead. One day when she was in seventh or eighth grade, Chelsea announced she was "going out" with a boy on the football team.

"What do you mean, *going out*?" I asked.

"You know, going out!"

"Do you mean that you're going on a date?" I asked her, while try-ing to imagine how middle school students would go anywhere at their age on limited funds and with no transportation. I was also flabbergasted! I may have liked boys at that age, but I had no clue about how to get their attention, let alone have a relationship!

"No—we sit together at lunch and walk to classes together."

"Oh!" I replied. "Hmmmm…so that constitutes a middle school relationship."

That first "relationship" lasted for a few months, but Chelsea seemed to be working at it much harder than the boy. We talked about being careful not to put too much effort into a boy that wasn't showing interest back. She found out later that he was spreading untrue rumors about what they had done together, much to her chagrin.

Lessons Learned

As a result of this boy's unkind behavior, Chelsea and I talked about why boys (let alone human beings!) make up stories that are hurtful—possibly because they are insecure and are desperate to feel better about themselves. We talked about how girls mature sooner than boys in many ways—that boys need extra time to figure out how to behave with girls, especially when it comes to respecting them. Chelsea was definitely hurt by the experience, but it helped her to make better choices later on.

The Older Boy

Chelsea's next relationship was with an older boy who lived in a city a few miles away and did not go to her school. (He was two years older, which worried me.) I think she met him through mutual friends and she was very smitten with him. In order for her to go to a movie with him alone versus meeting at the mall with other friends, he had to meet and be approved of by her dad. The boy wasn't up to the task, and I don't think he ever met her dad as long as they were "going out." Chelsea also learned over time that the boy was rather racist, which bothered her quite a bit.

Lessons Learned

She and I talked about the choices she had with this boy: to see him or not and whether to talk to him about his behavior. Chelsea told me over the next few months that she talked to him several times about his racist remarks and made requests of him about his behavior, but he never quite rose to the occasion. They stopped "going out" after several months, and she realizes today that it was a very good decision to leave him behind!

Leaving the Good Guy Behind

Do you remember the guy who wrote a song for Chelsea in chapter 4? Half way through ninth grade Chelsea's family decided to move a good thirty miles north. Chelsea and Andrew were faced with a big decision about what to do, since neither was old enough to drive. Andrew decided to "break up" with Chelsea because he knew that she would be at a new school with new people, and he knew it was unrealistic to think that they would continue to be able to see each other because of the distance.

Although she was crushed and was taking it personally, I suggested a different way for her to think about the break up—one that would boost her confidence and view the break up from a more positive perspective. I suggested that Andrew deserved a lot of credit for being so honest and authentic. (I assured her these traits were not very common in boys his age, and sometimes even older men!) I suggested that he was looking out for her in his own way. Chelsea and I talked about all the wonderful things that she had with this boy (respect, care and friendship), which she had not really had with other boys she had "hung out with" up to that point. I suggested to her that Andrew had helped her realize what wonderful things she could have in a relationship, and that nice boys really were out there. Because of him she had learned some of the qualities that were important to her and had experienced how well he had treated her, and she could carry that knowledge to her next relationship. Without him, she would not have gained this knowledge at this stage of her life. Even to this day she lets me know when she "learned a lot" from a relationship and how she will "make better choices" because of it. I smile every time I hear her say that, because it's a good reminder for me and my relationships too.

Lessons Learned

Although I couldn't relate to such crushes when I was her age, I got to learn a lot from her. Relationships have been a prevalent source of confidence-building discussions between the two of us. Many times I find myself thinking, "Who the heck am I?" I definitely don't have these things all figured out; I just tell her what I know or what experience I've had, and I try to help her think about the consequences, the impact, or the pros and cons, and I try to help her sort it out beforehand—if in fact I know beforehand. Sometimes—a lot of the time—I learn about things after the fact, when she's already made a choice. So, we sort through what worked, what didn't and how she would do things differently next time. At least she talks to me!

More Stories about Chelsea's Growing Self-Confidence

When Chelsea and her family moved, she was halfway through her freshman year in high school. Fortunately, they were moving to a more rural area with an excellent school system. Although she was a little uncomfortable starting a new school without knowing anyone, she also realized that any bad reputation, nicknames or labels that she may have accumulated in her old home town would be left behind. She had the opportunity to start over—to begin anew! She was very excited about that and we talked about it quite a bit before and after they moved.

Chelsea says...

After I moved to a new city and school, Paula just kept reminding me that I'm in a new place and I can make a new start. And, even though I'm in a new place, those unsupportive people that lived in my old neighborhood, they don't matter anymore. They're in my past.

Nonverbal Learning Disorder

As it turned out, moving gave Chelsea a fresh start educationally as well as socially. Chelsea has a nonverbal learning disorder that affects her ability to understand and carry out verbal instructions. When I first met her in fifth grade, she was in the Special Education program. In that school system, all students with any kind of disability or learning disorder were placed in the same Special Education classroom, so it's likely that few if any of them received the specialized attention they needed.

I know that I could see evidence that Chelsea's education in her former school system wasn't going as well as perhaps it could have. Occasionally, Chelsea would send me an e-mail or an instant message and I noticed her spelling and grammar were atrocious. In my replies I would ask, "Do you mean _____?" and correctly spell the word(s) that she misspelled in her message to me. It was my way of providing a quick spelling lesson, although it didn't really seem to take effect. But when Chelsea's family moved, things changed dramatically for the better. Chelsea and her learning disorder were understood far better in her new setting. She had a paraprofessional available to help her take and review notes and do what was needed to help Chelsea learn the material in the style that was most meaningful to her.

I specifically remember being at the community library with Chelsea one summer day. She was doing a book search on the computer for "Autism." (She loved working with the autistic students at her school and wanted to understand the disease better.) I stood nearby and watched her type in some keywords. Before she hit the RETURN key to do the search, she went back and corrected her spelling of the keywords. I said to her, "Wow, Chelsea—your spelling has really improved!"

She stopped what she was doing, looked directly at me and said, "This is the FIRST school where I have been expected to learn to spell correctly! No one ever expected me to spell properly before because I was in Special Ed!"

"Great!" was all I could reply. Her words said it all—she was grateful for being held to a quality standard for the first time in her school life and she was extremely proud of herself for rising to the occasion. You go girl!

Lessons Learned

I often felt a bit uncomfortable bringing Chelsea's unconventional sentence structures and misspelled words to her attention. I didn't want to point out a "failing" when I was supposed to be part of her support system. What I have learned is that Chelsea wants to succeed, spell words correctly and take pride in her performance. I assumed she was being given the proper training all along, but I was wrong. Chelsea was doing the best she could with the training and abilities she had.

A Caring Person, a Caring Career Path

Chelsea has quite a strong "Mama Bear" inside of her when it comes to protecting one of her family members, the children she babysits or the handicapped or autistic students she worked with in her high school. During a dinner at Boston Market when she was a high school junior, she excitedly told me about an autistic boy her age with whom she was paired during one class period every day during the semester. She gave him her undivided attention, developed a strong trusting relationship and helped him feel safe and comfortable with her. Because they had formed such a close bond, she was able to challenge him to be more independent. She was willing to develop a connection with the boy even though he was "different," could not talk and had seemed quite unreachable to the other staff and students. Chelsea reminded him of the things he already knew how to do rather than helping him complete the task or worse, do it for him. Chelsea feels she is truly contributing when she works with people who cannot do things for themselves, and especially people who cannot speak for themselves.

One day she announced that she knew what she wanted to do for a career. "I want to be the voice for kids that don't have a voice," she told me.

"What do you mean Chelsea?" I asked.

"I'm helping out in a Physically and Otherwise Health Impaired

(POHI) class in school and I love it!" she told me enthusiastically. She explained further that most of the students did not have the ability to talk and that she had learned to communicate with them through the sounds, movements or facial expressions they made. She also asked a lot of questions to help clarify what was going on with them. She told me she wanted to "speak for them" because they could not speak themselves.

I think Chelsea really felt drawn to working with these students because when she was a child and had experienced abuse, she felt "disabled," unable to get the help she needed or to take care of herself. Shortly before she graduated high school, she told me that she fully intended to invite all the POHI students to her Graduation Open House at the end of her senior year plus the autistic boy she worked with two years ago. I would have loved to have had the opportunity to see Chelsea interacting with these kids in school and I would absolutely love to see her working with people with special needs or helping patients with her occupational therapy skills a few years from now. I truly believe she will "be the change" in her future profession because it is a personal cause for her.

Lessons Learned
Chelsea excelled in working with kids that had significant special needs. Her ability to connect with and bond with these kids was often unmatched by any other student. She had been a student with special needs herself—to a lesser degree—but she understood what it felt like to be labeled or to have assumptions made about her abilities. She sees the true person, not just the disability. That is a real gift.

Different Messages

Chelsea tells a story about the difference between the messages she got from me and those she received from her then stepmom. She said:

"I always listened to my ex-stepmom. I always did. I never tried out for sports, because she used to always tell me the negative side of things. My stepmom would say, 'You know, you're going to have to train for three months for Track, Powder Puff (football) or Cheerleading.' She would tell me all these things to discourage me, including what I was thinking about studying in college. She told me, 'It's going to be really, really tough for you to be a special education teacher,' and all these other things. So I never tried out for any sports. But, just for the fun of it, in my junior year I tried out for the Powder Puff football team. The game takes place before Homecoming. I tried out mainly because Paula and I were talking about it. Paula told me, 'Oh, it would be so much fun! You know, you're going be a junior,' and all this other stuff. So my choice was based on the fun instead of whether I was good enough to try out. Paula went to my game, and she cheered me on, and it was the most fun I think I've had in my life."

Lessons Learned

Chelsea understands now that her former stepmom was trying to be supportive in her own way. She didn't want Chelsea to be disappointed, so she tried to steer her away from activities where that was a possibility. Over the time Chelsea's dad and this woman were married, I spoke to her several times. She was always supportive of my relationship with Chelsea and assured me that she and Chelsea's dad really trusted me and my decisions. Very recently, Chelsea told me that, after several years had passed, her ex-stepmom reached out to her on Facebook. She told Chelsea that she had always been a bit jealous of my relationship with Chelsea because it was largely unaffected by the family drama and didn't involve the authority component of parenting. I have to admit her jealousy was a surprise, but it made me realize that being a mentor is a truly unique kind of relationship.

Mentor as Job "Cheerleader"

One role I know I've played in Chelsea's life has been that of a job coach or, more accurately, job "cheerleader." Chelsea has been babysitting since she was about twelve for other people and has always taken her work very seriously. One summer, she had a full-time job caring for an eight-year-old boy and a three-year-old girl when she was only thirteen years old herself! She really loved those kids, especially the little girl, and often would want to look at little girl's clothes just for fun when we were at the mall. She made it her mission to make sure the little girl "used her words" rather than "baby talk" to communicate. She was concerned about the boy because he was overweight and didn't seem to want to go outside and play very much. She did her best to have a positive impact on both of her "charges."

The next year I made Chelsea color business cards on my computer so she could spread the word about her skills as a babysitter. She got a lot of positive feedback about the cards and she picked up some work as a result. Later, when she moved to a new neighborhood, I updated her business cards. She told me a story about being at a local park one day with her brothers. A woman was there with her two small children. Chelsea went up to the woman, commented how cute her children were and introduced herself. "Hi! I'm Chelsea and I babysit." She shook the woman's hand and gave her one of her business cards. The woman told Chelsea that she was "so professional" and she especially liked the firmness of her handshake. Needless to say, she got to babysit this woman's children!

Later in the year when Chelsea was looking for more work, she put a BABYSITTING flyer on her mailbox by the street. Within a few hours, she got a call from one of the neighbors. That girl has got quite an entrepreneurial spirit!

When she got older and more eligible to work for businesses, we made several trips to pick up job applications. We discussed the best approach to ensure that she got the information she needed and that her application ended up in the right hands. Her approach was something like this: "Hi, my name is Chelsea." (Extends hand for handshake.) "May I speak to the manager?" (Big smile.) "Are you accepting applications?" (Yes/No) "Thank you sir/ma'am!" (Big smile and exit.) I admit I am biased, but what confidence! What charisma! I was so proud of her! Atta girl Chelsea!

She tried for years to get a job outside of the babysitting realm just

to give her confidence a boost by proving that she could be successful in a business setting. When she was about sixteen, she almost got
hired at a Coney Island restaurant, but within a week they decided that
they had hired too many girls and she was unceremoniously "let go"
before she had actually started! We had a long talk about that one since
she had done everything she could to be professional, and the restaurant manager had done so many things to prove he was anything but
professional.

Towards the end of her senior year she was actively completing applications at the large mall near her house. We walked around the mall
one night and she picked up a few more applications. She had two mini-
interviews during her job tour and she was feeling very encouraged. As
we were leaving, she noticed a Justice for Girls store that specialized in
little girl's fashions. I said, "That would be perfect for you Chelsea!" She
agreed, but thought she would go there another time. I strongly encouraged her to pick up an application and—what do you know—they called
her a few days later for an interview! A week or so went by after the interview and she had not received a call-back. She called me the day after
her high school graduation and wondered if she should keep calling to
check on the status. She asked, "Does everybody get called back or is it
just the people who actually get hired?" Since she had left a message the
day before, I suggested she call every few days and I gently let her know
that it's not uncommon for only those who get hired to get a call-back.

She replied, "That's not right! If I was the person hiring I'd call everyone so they weren't just left wondering!"

I told her, "You're absolutely right Chelsea, but unfortunately compa-
nies don't always do that—not even in a professional employment setting."

I admit I was about ready to call that store myself and give the manager a piece of my mind. Instead, we talked about putting together her
résumé and she assured me, "Don't think this is going to stop me!"
A few hours later she called me back and said, "Guess who just called
me?" The manager of Justice for Girls returned her call, apologized for
the delay and offered her the job. She was ecstatic—the world of business
wanted her!

Lessons Learned

Those simple business cards gave Chelsea a huge ego boost! Chelsea loved handing them out and they truly set her apart from the average teenager looking for a babysitting job. She has never let the economy or "We're not hiring" or "You don't have enough experience" get in her way. She just tries even harder. Within the last year or so, after driving her around to pick up applications and watching her interact with store managers I asked her, "Where did you learn to shake hands like that? It's really a cool thing to do—people remember you because of it!"

She turned to me and smiled, "You taught me that Paula."

I was stunned, yet grinned from ear to ear. Another mentoring moment for the history books.

Life on Her Own

In her senior year (in the middle of a meal at Quizno's) Chelsea said, "I've been thinking a LOT about what life is going to be like after high school if I move out on my own...." Pause.

"Yes?" I encouraged.

"Even though my dad lets me have a lot of freedom, when I'm at home I have lots of boundaries and rules and structure that I'm expected to follow."

"Uh-huh," I said.

"I'm just wondering when I'm on my own what it's going to be like without the boundaries and rules."

I thought about what she said for a minute. She sounded like she was a little scared about the future. Was she afraid she would make bad choices, hurt herself or disappoint others? I decided encouragement was required.

"Well, I think you have a great capacity to take care of yourself and make good choices Chelsea. I don't want you to sell yourself short!" I said to her, "You told me just a few weeks ago that you would like to go to a Christian college because you would be surrounded by people who are making good choices, which will help you make good choices too. The same goes for living on your own. You pick the people that will support you in your life—people who are making good choices. You can do that now and also later when you're living on your own."

She seemed to be listening. I decided some reality might help. "Sure—when people go off to college, they kind of go crazy for a while because they're on their own for the first time. But if you're paying for your own tuition and your grades aren't good, that can grab your attention!"

"Yeah!" she agreed.

"But then you realize you're in charge and you've got to make it work—and you do," I told her.

I think because her older sister didn't choose college and is barely making ends meet living with her boyfriend, Chelsea feels extra responsibility to perform and be successful in college and in life. She needed some encouragement and I did my best to supply what she needed.

Lessons Learned

Interestingly, we just had a similar conversation and Chelsea is now twenty-one. She is leaving for what could be more than a year away at a vocational school on the other side of the state. She is stressing about whether she'll make friends, get good enough grades, what it will be like to live in a dormitory with one or more roommates, whether she'll make good choices or be swayed by peer pressure. Pretty much everything under the sun surfaced while she got it all off her chest. My part in the conversation was to remind her of the challenges that she had already overcome and the good choices she learned to make. She kept bringing up the "what ifs" and I listened and reminded her that she could do this and that she knows how to ask for help. Going away to school is a big confident step for Chelsea. She really wants this opportunity and is proud of herself for taking it. She wants to go on to Occupational Therapy school afterwards. Watching Chelsea take this step is a really proud moment for me as her mentor.

Final Thoughts

Have you figured out that mentoring goes both ways? It is an opportunity for both people to share insights and learning and to respect another generation's perspective. The thoughts and observations that Chelsea shares with me absolutely amaze me on a regular basis. You can't help but become each other's biggest fan club!

Reflection: Your Mentee's Self-Confidence

Take a few moments to reflect on these questions:

1. How do you think you will help build your mentee's confidence?

   _____

   _____

   _____

   _____

   _____

   _____

2. How do you think she will help build yours?

   _____

   _____

   _____

   _____

   _____

   _____

CHAPTER EIGHT

When the Going Gets Tough

Often the most loving thing we can do when a friend is in pain is to share the pain—to be there even when we have nothing to offer except our presence and even when being there is painful to ourselves.
—M. Scott Peck—

When Chelsea was about fourteen and in eighth grade, her mom moved out of the state. Chelsea was wrestling with a strained relationship with her anyway, but having her mother move across the country without so much as a backward glance was very upsetting to Chelsea and her three siblings.

That same year Chelsea gave me a framed poem she had written. She had typed it out on a computer using red ink and printed it out for me. It was entitled *Screaming.* She had never told me before that she had any interest in writing poetry, and as I read it I noticed she really had some talent! I was also a bit disturbed with the poem's content, even though I didn't completely understand it all. I didn't feel comfortable asking her what it meant or why she wrote a poem with that title. I thanked her for her gift nonetheless.

Several years later Chelsea explained the meaning behind the poem. "The very first poem I ever wrote was on my birthday, and my mom didn't call me to wish me a happy birthday. The first one was about screaming. It's because my body and my mind and my heart and everything was screaming inside because she didn't call. She left me hanging." She went on to say, "Ever since then my hand and my pencil were best friends."

She told me she wrote poetry as a sort of therapy, so over the years I've purchased blank journals for her to unload her thoughts or feelings when she needs or wants to do so. When she was feeling particularly down or "stuck" I would say to her, "Have you thought about writing some poetry?" More often than not, she is glad I reminded her.

Mentoring programs are in place for a reason. A child is missing a consistent, positive role model in her life and her behavior demonstrates that she is at risk of making poor decisions or has already made some poor decisions. Your mentee may come from poor, middle class or wealthy circumstances. A surplus of money does not guarantee a healthy, functioning family structure. Your mentee may come from a single parent family where the parent or guardian at home is too busy to spend time with the child or incapable of being a positive role model. Your mentee may live with a relative who didn't know what they were getting into when they accepted responsibility for this child. Your mentee may come from a foster family where personal attention is at a premium. Your mentee may be living in a juvenile detention facility because she broke the law. The adults in this child's life (if there are some actively-involved adults) may have issues relating to substance abuse, unemployment and poor living conditions. These "realities" could be part of your mentee's world. She may not even realize her home life is "different" than anyone else's—how could she know? Your job as a mentor is to focus on the child and not let her circumstances define her potential or her capacity to flourish.

In this chapter I clarify your role as a mentor during the inevitable tough times that you and your mentee will face together. I provide a significant number of "support tools" to help you navigate some tough situations. Finally, I share some personal stories about challenging times that I have helped Chelsea navigate in the hope that they are helpful to you.

Your Role as a Mentor During Tough Times

Let's face some facts. People do the best they can with what they know. Adults who have children were not all meant to be caring mothers and fathers. Children do not always get the parents they deserve or the help they need to thrive. It takes a village to raise a child. Mentors are a critical part of the "village" albeit not as family members. Ninety-five per cent of the time I have spent with Chelsea, her family has been very welcoming to me. However, I'm still an outsider in comparison to immediate family members.

As a mentor, you get to be involved at arm's length, which can be convenient and distressing all at the same time. You will hear about the problems, but have little influence in making them go away for your mentee. Certainly, there were and are times that I hear Chelsea's version of something that happened at home and it has been disturbing, whether it was something she had gotten in trouble for or a disagreement with her father or former stepmother.

I've never felt qualified to make judgments as a parent because I have never been a parent, nor am I in this relationship. I am just an outside adult, and I am only hearing Chelsea's side of the story. I certainly was her most supportive listener, and wanted to side with her version. I wanted to be supportive, and I, in a lot of ways, believed her version was true, and that the rest of the world misunderstood her. But I also know the dynamics of families, and I understand that she's probably going to spin the story so that she looks as good as possible.

Still, I have felt frustrated and angry a number of times because I am just an observer. I have no power. I get to see Chelsea a couple of hours a week, hear whatever is going on, and then send her back home. In reality, I probably won't talk to her again until the following week. She could be a completely different girl the following week and be as happy as can be. She might say, "Oh that's not a big deal anymore," or, "That got resolved as soon as I got home after we talked." I know the volatility associated with being a girl and being a teenager; something that was really, really horrible today could be nonexistent tomorrow.

So, it was and continues to be occasionally frustrating to be an outsider looking in. On other days, it works just fine.

As a mentor you are offering her an oasis in what could be a challenging home life. Even so, you may encounter some tough situations and it may be very distracting to you because you may want to rescue her and fix or change this little girl's living situation. There are health and safety situations where rescue may be called for, and I discuss that in this chapter. But what I want to clarify for you is what your mentor "job" is and is not during tough times.

Support "Tools" for When the Going Gets Tough

Let me be brutally honest: I am not a parent, counselor, minister or Dr. Phil! I read a good amount, attend educational and personal growth events, have worked with a life coach and have seen a counselor now and then. Twenty plus years ago I learned some ways to relate to children through working with them in schools and the YMCA. Within the last ten years, I have been a mentor, a Sunday school teacher, a repeat volunteer at local Challenge Day programs at middle and high schools, and a volunteer adult facilitator connected to a Teen Peace Circle program at a church, a teen leadership "coach" and an elementary school tutor. I never planned to be an expert with children and I am definitely not one today. I just pay attention to what I read and hear, and try to apply it when it seems appropriate.

As a mentor, I am certain that for every moment I am a good, respectful listener there is another moment where I let my ego take over and "tell her" what she should do. It pains me to admit that, but it's true. (Chelsea can confirm this!) But—as the Japanese proverb teaches us—fall seven times, stand up eight. I'm not perfect and chances are, neither are you. We must be human! That works very well in mentoring.

Over the years when I deal with challenging topics with young people (or anyone!), I pull out some support tools that seem to help keep the relationship and conversation going rather than shut things down.

I'm sharing them with you so that you have more tools for your own "toolbox." They are in no particular order. They are not solutions for every situation, but I think they may be helpful in some cases. You may recognize some of these strategies from earlier chapters, but the following table pulls them together—along with some new strategies—as a comprehensive resource.

I also encourage you to review the resources on my blog www.YouthMentorIdeas.com, which provides additional information for you to use when and if you need it.

Support Tools in Tough Situations	
Actively listen to her.	• Face her. • Softly look into her eyes if she is comfortable with you doing so. • Nod your head so she knows you're listening. • Let her be the talker. • Verbally respond if appropriate. • Let her know you are interested, alert and supportive with your body language.
Remind her of all her positive traits—that she's good/strong/brave/talented/kind.	• "You sound really proud of yourself for getting that A on your report card!" • "You were really brave to let your dad know that he wasn't giving you quality time.'" • "You were so strong to stand up to that boy in school and tell him to leave you alone!" • "You are so good with babies; you must be a great babysitter!"
What do you think?	Children may rely on adults to make the "best" decisions or choices and that may make sense in many situations. But in situations where adults are not making good choices, children are confused, possibly scared and don't know where to turn for support. She may or may not trust your opinion or advice anyway. As a mentor, it's easy to tell her what to do or how to do it. But does that help her self-confidence? Does it help her problem-solving skills? Every once in a while, try out "What do you think?" when she's sorting out what to do or what not to do. You may both be surprised at what she comes up with!

Support Tools in Tough Situations	
How do you feel about that?	This question may need to wait until you and your mentee get to know each other and are developing some trust. Feelings are not always understood enough to express them and/or she may not be allowed to express her feelings at home. When she seems "full of feelings," ask her, "How do you feel about that?" and see how she responds. Don't push it; just bring the question up in normal conversation every once in a while.
How's that working for you?	Dr. Phil is pretty famous for this question. It seems to work for older kids because they are more able to reflect on how something affects them and whether it is working or not. Once they can get past the upset to think about whether it's a positive or negative in their lives, they can start making choices about whether they want it to continue or not. Eventually you can help them sort things through and start to problem solve.
I want to make sure I understand. Is it okay if I ask you some questions?	You are showing respect for her by wanting to clearly under-stand her, yet you are not assuming it's okay to ask clarifying questions. Always get permission to probe further.
Write it down.	If your mentee is struggling with something at home or school or in life, she might find it useful to write it down in a journal, a poem or even in song lyrics. Let her know the writing is just for her and nobody else; she can rip it to shreds or show it to others if she likes. Chelsea has used poetry as her form of personal "therapy" at different times in her life. Perhaps your mentee might find this useful!
What do you need from me right now?	When your mentee is really struggling, but not necessarily communicating what is going on for her, this question can truly help. She may just want to vent, cry, listen to the radio or not say a thing! Asking this question lets her know she is in charge and you're there to listen if she wants to talk. Depending on the situation, you might offer her a few choices to help her: "Do you want a hug?" "Do you want to talk about that?" "Do you want me to keep quiet?" Sometimes a comforting hand on her shoulder might just be enough but it's a good idea to ask if it's okay first.

Support Tools in Tough Situations	

Encourage her to make requests of adults.
 	
Confronting adults may NOT be recommended in all circumstances depending on what kind of relationship there is between your mentee and the adult. Explore how comfortable she is about approaching an adult in her life. Often times, she may see something as impossible because she feels she is not important. A little encouragement can go a long way.
	Some examples (not all inclusive):
	
	• If she wants more quality time with a busy parent, encourage her to ask the adult to schedule a date on the calendar for an ice cream appointment, a "date" night or a special walk together. This is an alternative to blaming the parent or assuming the parent doesn't care about her.
	
	• Encourage her to ask her teacher if she can talk about some of her math homework that is causing her problems rather than getting more frustrated and getting more failing grades.
	
	• Suggest to her that she ask her parent for a "family meeting" so everyone is present and recurring problems are discussed with all those involved, rather than feeling out of control and resentful.
	
	• Embolden her to meet with a coach to explain an absence rather than assuming she's off the team, "doomed," etc.
	
	• If she has an issue with how an adult in her life is behaving toward her (this may work the best for a preteen and teenager):
	
	  1. Try to find out what happened to cause her upset so you can help determine if she alone can handle this issue.
	
	  2. Establish where her insecurity comes from (e.g., Because of poor self-esteem? Because she feels she might get physically hurt? Because the person is an adult and it could be considered disrespectful?).
	
	  3. If it sounds like something that is too much for her to handle on her own, ask her if she'd like help to involve another adult who would be supportive (parent, relative, teacher, counselor, caseworker, etc.). Offer to speak to that adult with her so she is not alone. If it sounds like something she might be able to handle with some encouragement, talk about standing up for her own physical boundaries and personal treatment. Remind her that it's okay to let others know what does not work for her and what does work for her. Let her know people need clear, simple messages, for example "Grandpa—when you tickle me it makes me very uncomfortable. Please don't tickle me—I don't like that." "Uncle Jack—when you swear around me it makes me uncomfortable. I don't like swearing—can you please stop doing it around me?" Role play the situation several times so she can practice her new behavior with you playing the offending adult.

Support Tools in Tough Situations	
Encourage her to make requests of her peers and/or siblings. *Sometimes, children (and adults!) can make up stories about "why things are so" with very little fact or evidence. "If my friend ignores me, it's because she doesn't like me anymore." "If my boyfriend didn't call me, he must be mad at me." Support her in asking questions to get some answers.*	Some examples (not all inclusive!): • If a boy at school makes fun of her every day, encourage her to confront him. "John—I do not appreciate you making fun of me and I want you to stop right now. If you don't stop it I will report it to the principal." Role play this scenario if appropriate. • If a girlfriend suddenly seems distant and unfriendly, encourage her to talk to her friend directly. "Mary—I've noticed that we don't eat lunch together or talk much anymore. I really miss hanging out with you and it makes me feel sad that things have changed between us. I want to be friends with you. Can you help me understand what's going on?" Role play this scenario if appropriate. • If a boyfriend makes inappropriate comments about her figure in front of others, remind her that if she is uncomfortable with his behavior that is all that matters. If he says she is "over-reacting" he is not respecting her. Encourage her to confront him and use "I" statements (speak from own experience versus blaming), for example, "John—when you talk about my body in front of your friends, it makes me feel very uncomfortable and disrespected. I want you to stop doing that. I don't like it." Role play this scenario if appropriate.
Do you want some feedback?	Teenagers are often viewed as over-sized kids that need to be "controlled." Plenty of adults in their lives make it a practice of telling them what to do, when to do it and how to do it well. Certainly they need some guidance, but wouldn't it be amazing if an adult asked a teenager—quite respectfully — "Do you want some feedback?" As a mentor, you are her friend, supporter and nonjudgmental listener. By NOT assuming she "needs" your unsolicited wisdom, it sends a huge message to her. "I respect you. You get to choose whether you want to hear more from me. If you want to just complain out loud, that's okay. I am not like 'all those other adults.' You have control over how this conversation goes." This is a tough tool to implement—believe me! But it really does work and it builds trust between the two of you.

Support Tools in Tough Situations	
Teenagers are young adults with less experience.	When I worked with teens at a local Unity church outside of Detroit, my friend Mark Van der Gaag—the Teen Director at the time and a certified life coach—told me that he didn't look upon the teens as kids, but rather as "young adults with less experience." He further explained, "Teenagers can make the same decisions as you and me, only they have less experience in life." In other words, they could (and would!) make mistakes while they learned and explored—and sometimes with major consequences. (We all were teenagers once!) As a result of my work with Mark and the teens and things I have learned on my own, here are some principles I keep in mind as a mentor working with a teenager: • Recognize teenagers can make "adult decisions" at any moment. • It is foolish to think of them as little "children" who will not take risks. • In most cases they already have adult bodies and they are all about establishing their independence, testing boundaries and potentially exploring their sexuality. • If she doesn't decide her boundaries ahead of time, she will be hard pressed to set them in the heat of the moment. Discuss what boundaries she desires regarding boys, alcohol, drugs, skipping school and so on. Role play if it makes sense. Make her aware that drugs and alcohol severely compromise any boundaries she has set for herself. • Risk-taking is part of the teenage territory—for better or for worse! • Make sure she is aware of multiple choices in order to make good decisions. Talk about adult topics whenever it seems appropriate. • Make sure she has information available to her to make good decisions: printed information, websites and phone numbers (see www.YouthMentorIdeas.com). • Make sure she knows you believe she can and does make good decisions. Remind her of this all the time. • Make sure she knows you are a safe, nonjudgmental adult she can tell things to even if she slips up now and then. • Make sure she knows you care for her very much and you want the best for her.

Real Life Stories: Lessons Learned from Tough Times

For the most part, my time with Chelsea has been pretty "smooth sailing." But when family dynamics started to take their toll in the form of drama, alcohol and making poor choices I didn't always feel capable or skillful. But that is because I had slipped into a "rescue, fix or change" frame of mind versus being a reliable, supportive mentor. The personal stories below give you a firsthand view of mentoring plus the lessons that Chelsea and I learned as a result of these experiences.

When a Parent or Guardian Wants You to "Talk To Her"

The summer after I met Chelsea, just before she turned twelve, her dad signed her and her three siblings up for the local Boys & Girls Club summer program. Shortly after the summer began, I got a call from her dad. "Can you talk to Chelsea? She's discovered boys at the Boys & Girls Club and is going to get suspended from camp if she doesn't straighten up!" He was a single parent at the time. I happened to be the female adult that he felt he could approach. I admit this was new territory for me. I was a single adult with no children of my own and it had been years since I worked with kids on a regular basis.

"What?" I asked him to explain. He told me the program director had called him at work to report that Chelsea had been running the halls with some boys in the program against Club rules and had been seen licking one boy's ear in an effort to get his attention. I found out she was suspended for a few days from the summer program. Again, her dad pleaded with me, *"Please talk to her!"*

Man, was I feeling ill-equipped! Child-rearing experience was not exactly dripping from me at that time, but I was willing to take my best shot. I requested an extra night to meet with her and confirmed with him that she knew he had called me about the problem. I wanted to make sure I wasn't getting in between Chelsea and her father, or breaking any confidences between them.

As Chelsea climbed into my SUV that evening, I wondered how we were going to talk about "it" if I wasn't supposed to probe. As it turned out, though, she was *quite* repentant for her wayward behavior, and blurted out, "I REALLY let my dad down and I TOTALLY understand why I got in trouble at the Boys & Girls Club."

"Uh-huh," I said.

"I'm REALLY embarrassed about what I did and I'm NEVER going to do that again!"

"Okay...," I said, nodding my head. Problem solved! She had already told me several times that she was a "Daddy's girl" and really hated to disappoint her father.

Chelsea and I talked a little bit about why she behaved the way she did (to get attention) and brainstormed about different ways to make friends—which didn't involve ear licking! Between her dad talking to her, having to face me for an extra visit because of her behavior, and her own embarrassment, Chelsea seemed to learn from her mistakes and was ready to change her ways. The best part was, all I did was listen, ask clarifying questions and be supportive. Cool!

Lesson Learned

Allowing her time to think about what she had done was helpful. The fact that Chelsea knew we were getting together sooner than usual because of the problem at the Boys & Girls Club must have weighed heavily on her. I think it is very important to have a parent tell my mentee when he or she has spoken to me directly about her behavior so there are no surprises. I never wanted to make Chelsea feel I was sneaking behind her back to gather information from her dad, otherwise the trust we had built would have been broken.

More Requests from Dad

Another time Chelsea's dad asked me to talk to her was a time we now refer to as "The Skating Rink Incident." When Chelsea was about thirteen, she liked to go to the local skating rink on the weekend. Her dad would typically drop her off and then pick her up later at an agreed

Chelsea says...

I remember one time Paula picked me up from the Boys & Girls Club and I'm wearing this sleazy little tank top, itty bitty little boogie shorts and some little sandals or something like that. I got in the car and she just looked at me and said, "Chelsea, I love you but I'm really worried about you. You are acting like a very different girl than the one I know. I love and I care about you, but I'm really concerned about you. I'm concerned about your well-being."

I was in the sixth grade and I'd just started paying attention to the boys who seemed to like me. I was starting to get little mosquito bites—I already went through puberty—well, they were a little bit more than mosquito bites. I figure that's probably why the boys liked me, because I was a sixth grader that had big boobs.

I remember going to the Boys & Girls Club and they would snap my bra and I thought it was really cool because they actually noticed that I wore bras (at my age). Everyone always made fun of me in elementary school.

But I hated Paula talking to me that time because it felt like she started telling me how to live my life. But at the same time, I saw it a little different because the way that she approached it was "I love you, Chelsea. I love you and I care about you. I see that you're hurting and I see that you're getting influenced by peer pressure. You don't need to do that because your friends who are going to be your friends love you. The friends that you call friends at this place are not really your friends—they don't want the best for you."

I'll never forget that. I went through a lot of hell in the sixth grade—it was just a whirlwind. I'm really surprised I'm not pregnant by now because I've gone through so many bad experiences—especially when I hit rock bottom last summer.

So I've really learned so much from all these people, including Paula. I've learned to love myself. You know what I've also learned? I have a voice. I have a voice to say no. I have a voice to say yes and I have a voice that is strong and powerful that anybody can hear.

upon time. Chelsea's dad called me one night and told me that another problem had come up on the subject of boys and it involved the skating rink. He sounded like he felt he was losing control of his daughter. He wanted to give me a "heads up" on what had transpired before I saw Chelsea on our normal weekly get together. Once again, he was hoping I would "talk to her."

A panicky feeling swept over me and I thought desperately, *"Whaaaat? Why is he calling me again? What am I going to say to her? I hardly have MEN figured out, let alone BOYS!"*

Rather than share my innermost thoughts and feelings, I put on my MENTOR hat and calmly suggested that he and I meet at the Big Boy restaurant half way between our homes to talk. When we sat down at the restaurant, he admitted to me that he had heard some bad things about the adult supervision at the skating rink and he was a little uncomfortable letting Chelsea go there. One night after he dropped her off, he made a surprise return to the skating rink to check on things himself. There he found as he told me "a sea of twelve- and thirteen-year-olds making out" in subdued lighting, with no adult supervisor in sight! Unfortunately (or fortunately) for Chelsea, he found her sitting on the lap of a boy in a solid lip lock amongst many others doing the same thing. No one—including Chelsea and the boy—saw him coming! He waded through the numerous young couples, grabbed his daughter and practically carried her out of the rink amidst her protests and his own anger and frustration. I found out she was clearly in the doghouse at home, and he didn't know what to do. He was especially concerned about the message she was sending others, let alone the dangers of young people getting sexual at an ever earlier age.

One of the things I wanted to clarify was the way she was being taught at home (or at church) regarding boys and appropriate behavior versus what my own perspective was on the topic. I listened to the story over sips of lemonade, clarified the punishment she was already facing (grounding, no more roller rink, no phone use), and asked him how he handled the subject of boys, sex and ground rules at his house so I knew what the boundaries were. I learned that he had very frank talks with his daughters because he didn't want them to make poor choices. I would describe him as a modern Southern Baptist dad. He told me he had discussions with both his daughters that stressed that abstinence is highly recommended and should pregnancy occur, "You will raise the baby yourself—don't expect your dad to!" Alrighty then! I again verified that she knew we were meeting and what we were talking about so I wasn't breaking any confidences between Chelsea and her dad.

Chelsea and I met the next night, had dinner and in order to get to THE TOPIC before the end of the night, I asked an innocent question, "How was your weekend Chelsea?" (I've come to notice that she always hits me with THE BIG TOPICS while I'm driving so I can't possibly maintain eye contact or we will be at risk of crashing. This was no exception!) In the next few minutes she blurted out everything she had to say on the topic—she was clearly waiting to get it off her chest. She told me, "Everyone *knows* that you go the skating rink to make out. Nobody goes there to *skate*." She admitted she did not know the boy she was kissing—she had just met him that night—but that was not uncommon at the skating rink. She had no business sitting in his lap either!

She clearly had plenty of time to dwell on her behavior after her dad carried her out of the rink and before she saw me. She had concluded that: she had broken a trust she had with her dad, she was very sorry for breaking a trust and she didn't know what it would take to repair the relationship, but she was working on it; she got caught up with peer pressure to make out with a boy she didn't know, that it was a bad decision and she was worried about her reputation because of it; she lost her roller blades because she and her dad had left so abruptly—but she understood why they wouldn't be replaced; she felt she had let me down with her behavior; she wished she had never gone to the skating rink at all. Phew! I didn't know if she was telling me what she thought I wanted to hear or if she really believed what she had just shared. Either way, she had spent a lot of brain cells on the topic!

I listened intently to her story. (I admit, I was thinking about how my life as a thirteen-year-old girl had been far less "worldly" than hers, but this was the new Millennium!) I tried to respond appropriately. "So it sounds like you had some time to think about it and will have a different way of doing things next time."

She agreed wholeheartedly! We talked about how the skating rink episode could affect her reputation at school. She worried about the "slut" label she hated so much and how this behavior might feed into that label. We talked about why she participated with the other kids. "He was older, and really attractive," Chelsea told me. "He, you know, he just made me feel like the world, because I was this little girl in seventh grade that a high school boy wanted to make out with." We also talked about whether the boy she was kissing really "knew" who the *real* Chelsea was as a result of what had happened. I tried to make my questions open-ended, just to get a handle on what she was thinking. Did he like her at all? Did he respect her? Did she know anything about him other than how he kisses? Does kissing make a relationship? What would she like a boy that kisses her to think about her as a person? I tried to ask a lot of questions so she could come up with her own conclusions. Even today she is still a bit mortified by the memory, but we sort of chuckle about it anyway.

Chelsea reflected, "That whole year (while she was grounded), I really realized what I was doing. Now that I think of it, I don't really remember it—it was just one thing. But at that time I was really ashamed of myself." She definitely has learned a lot in hindsight from The Skating Rink Incident—but she didn't really appreciate the "favor" her dad did for her at the time. After she and I talked I asked her, "Have you heard from this boy since then?"

"Yeah—he tried calling my house and my dad answered the phone!" Smiling, she mimicked her dad in a gruff voice, "Who is this??? You're not talking to my daughter!" Chelsea told me she did not plan to see the boy again.

I asked her, "Are you okay with that?"

She told me, "Oh yeah—I didn't even *know* him." Another hurdle cleared.

Chelsea says...

I didn't always want to listen to Paula. She kept telling me things and I was like, "Okay, you can shut up now! You're lecturing me like everyone else does." If I had only listened to her then. Because from then on, I sort of went downhill and started to really act inappropriately at school. I wanted to feel like somebody who was more important. I started doing everything I could to get a boy to like me or a girl to be my friend. I kind of lost respect for myself.

Lesson Learned

Again, making sure the parent tells her we have talked is important. This was a big event in Chelsea's young life and her self-esteem took flight and crashed in a small window of time. Treading softly was important. Her dad is a man and was protective of his little girl. To complicate things, Chelsea was a cute, thirteen-year-old girl with a well-developed body amongst a crowd of boys and girls with raging hormones. My role was to try to listen as a woman, with care and support. I wanted to understand where she was coming from as a young girl. I wanted to help her reflect on the boy, her choices, her reputation and—most importantly—how she would choose next time. I didn't prevent it from happening, but I helped sort it out.

Abuse

As a mentor, it is possible you could become aware that your mentee has suffered some type of abuse in the past or perhaps even in the present. The caseworker may have given you a "heads up" or you may have gathered over time that your mentee experienced physical, sexual or emotional abuse based on what she says (or doesn't say) or what you observe. Hopefully she has either gotten counseling *or* is getting counseling, and the offending person is out of her life. Even so, emotional scars may still be very prevalent and they may surface for reasons neither you nor she understand. No matter what happened, your approach is the same—be consistent, nonjudgmental, supportive and caring. The decision to share that chapter of her life with you is up to her. Probing for more information or assuming you know how she's feeling have no place here. It's her call if she wants to talk to you or not.

It took Chelsea *three* years to confide in me about some abuse she experienced as a young child. Whether I ever learned "what happened" was not the issue and it was never my goal to find out. The fact that I was available to her as a mentor when she was ready to talk and that we had developed a trusting relationship was worthy of celebration. What a compliment she gave me! What a brave girl she is! That experience convinced me—beyond anything else—that mentoring makes a difference. The important thing to remember is you don't know when you'll make a difference—so hang in there so that the miracles can unfold.

Chelsea says...

My most important memory was when I told Paula that I was molested. It was the most heartwarming, compassionate, closeness we've ever had, because I told her what had happened, and we shared a closeness. We shared the love. I mean, it truly showed me how much she cared about me, because she didn't break down and go, "Oh, I'm so sorry!" like everybody else has done. Her heart was out for me. She didn't just pity me like the others. She was feeling how I felt and it was the most amazing feeling ever. I finally felt comforted. I didn't feel like somebody was feeling sorry for me. It wasn't like all those lawyers, and all the people at Protective Services, and all the people I had to deal with at the court. I wanted to tell all of them, "I know you're sorry...but that's not going to do anything for me." I just need someone's true, honest comfort.

Lessons Learned
You can't rush connection or her willingness to share the biggest secrets of her life. Things will unfold if and when she wants them to, on her own timeline. I learned that providing a safe place for her to share or not share is what mentoring is all about. We focused on the present, not the past or the future. She wrote the agenda.

Alcohol

I would be lying if I told you I did not experiment with alcohol when I was a teenager. I guess I expected to encounter drinking at some point in my relationship with Chelsea, but well into her teens! The truth is I was secretly hoping it would never happen and that my influence as a mentor would support her in being a perfect, alcohol-free teenager. Think again!

When Chelsea was in eighth or ninth grade, she mentioned that she had been invited to a home party after a football game, and she knew the party would include alcohol. She told me she decided in advance that it would be a bad place for her to go. She admitted she was curious about what she had heard about drinking (how it made you feel, how "goofy" people behaved), but she figured she would rather not go and thus avoid the risk.

My first thought was, "Omigod, they start drinking this soon?" Then, I came to my senses and reminded myself that the same thing was going on when I was her age, but I had avoided it until I was about sixteen.

I realized that my experience of Chelsea is limited to the time we spend together and what she chooses to share with me. The fact that she trusted me enough to mention the party with the potential for alcohol—and that she was telling me she had decided not to go because of it—was rather huge. I applauded her for thinking ahead and making a good choice. Whenever it is appropriate, I remind Chelsea that deciding where she stands on different issues ahead of time is critical. Whether it's alcohol, drugs, sex, smoking or cutting school, she's got to make a decision now so she will be better prepared later when faced with other people who want her to make a different choice. She has the teachings of her church and family pulling her on one side and peer pressure and boys pulling on the other. Both are powerful influences, but I think that for the most part she puts some good thought into the choices and actions she takes.

In her later years in high school, she admitted to getting into trouble with her parents because she had been drinking with a friend and the friend's older brother (who bought the alcohol). Her younger brother had "turned her in" when he witnessed her drunken state. Again, she offered the information to me when she didn't have to, which I thanked her for. By the time we talked, three weeks had passed and she had decided by then that she would not have anything to do with alcohol again.

I asked her what had happened. She claimed it was her first time drinking and she had done "about four shots." I asked her if she remembered anything from the evening.

"Most of it. I think I was pretty much in control," she told me.

"Yeah, right," I thought. I calmly suggested to her that four shots of alcohol combined with a one-hundred-and-ten-pound body sounded pretty lethal to me. (She eventually admitted she had learned that in Health class.) I suggested—as casually as possible—that perhaps she was not aware of everything that happened that night. I told her that alcohol could have wiped out some of the evening. I asked about the older brother that was supplying the alcohol; did she know him well? (Read: "Did he take advantage of you?" I tried to stay calm and collected, but it was hard!) She thought he was trustworthy since he was the brother of her girlfriend. "I hope so!" I thought.

Rather than risk sounding like another preachy adult by telling her all the stuff she already knew about drinking, I decided to take a different approach and talk about my first experience with drinking. I told Chelsea that when I had too much to drink, I was sixteen years old and at a party given by a guy who was known for the alcohol at his parties. It was a hot summer night and he had a big Igloo cooler filled with lemonade and vodka. Everybody was drinking and having a great time. All I tasted was the lemonade and I was thirsty! Before I knew it, the room was swimming and I was sitting on some guy's lap with my sense of control slipping away (okay, it was gone)! One of the boys decided to pull me over to a secluded cubby hole in the basement to test my boundaries. I explained to Chelsea that fortunately for me, I had some girlfriends watching over me.

The bad news was that a boy I hardly knew decided to take advantage of my drunken state before my girlfriends rescued me. The worst news was that I really don't know how long it took my friends to find me. My story got Chelsea's attention.

Chelsea thought the people she was drinking with could be trusted. I told her I sincerely hoped that was true. But I suggested to her, "When you add alcohol to any situation, you don't behave 'normally' and sometimes your inhibitions slip away and you do things you wouldn't be proud of later." She had put herself in a very vulnerable situation. I told her it was something to seriously consider for the future. She assured me that she didn't plan on drinking again because it posed a trust issue (again) with her parents and she was embarrassed that she had withheld the information from me for so long. I told her I supported her decision and I forgave her for holding off on telling me. I told her I knew she would be faced with these decisions again and again and that she had the capacity to make good decisions on her own. But, knowing where she stood in advance is always a good place to start.

Chelsea says...

When I experimented with alcohol and was wondering whether I should tell Paula about it I think it was just another one of those, "I feel guilty, I don't want Paula to talk to me about it, but I know she will. She cares about me way too much to let me drink," type of thing. So, Paula and I had a nice long talk, and her perspective changed a lot of the ways I thought about things. When I talk to her about tough topics I know I'm not going to lose her respect, and I want her trust. Her trust in me is very important.

Lesson Learned

The reality of working with teenagers is that they want to fit in, they will experiment and they sometimes repeat their mistakes. As a mentor, your goal should be to keep the lines of communication open and to help address problems or decisions—ideally before they occur. (Good luck on that one!) Just keep being a nonjudgmental, caring adult friend.

If you help build her self-confidence to make good decisions indepen-
dently, you've accomplished a lot! If she slips up now and then, just
meet her where she is and "rinse and repeat."

Car Accident and Feeling Out of the Loop

One evening just before Chelsea turned eighteen and started her senior
year in high school, we got together on our regular night. I expected to
hear about her successfully completing her Road Test for her driver's
license and about some social event she had been looking forward to.

Instead she told me a pretty upsetting story. She showed me a large
scrape on her forehead, one of the injuries she had sustained in a car
accident the previous week. She had been walking home from a small
lake near her house and a guy she was acquainted with stopped and
offered her a ride home. She accepted, climbed in his SUV and put on
her seat belt. They were catching up on each others' lives as they drove
north on a road by her house. She noticed he missed a left turn into her
subdivision and continued on the road where it turned from asphalt to
gravel. He was driving pretty fast while he was talking animatedly to
her and suddenly he lost control of the truck. She later learned that the
truck rolled over a few times and came to rest against a tree. During the
rolling her seat belt either came unlatched or it broke. She must have hit
her head during the rolling and was left unconscious. She later pieced
together what had happened based on what the driver, police and ambulance personnel told her.

As it turned out, her friend was driving without a license or insurance. When the accident occurred, he pulled Chelsea out of the truck
and carried her in the direction of his brother's house which was in
the vicinity. Two girls in a golf cart happened to drive by and offered
to take them there. Once at his brother's, he asked his brother to take
Chelsea home. She said she was not entirely conscious at the time, but
arrived home with a large knot on her forehead, bleeding and very
unsteady. Her grandmother was there to receive her and was very upset with what she saw. Chelsea's dad arrived and shortly thereafter

the police and an ambulance arrived. Chelsea's purse had been left in the overturned truck and the police found it and were looking for the people that had been in the accident. They were able to track her down using identification in her purse. Chelsea and her dad were taken to the hospital by ambulance to have her examined. The guy that drove the truck was arrested for leaving the scene of an accident and driving without a license or insurance.

Chelsea was on a lot of pain medication when I saw her that night. She was angry with herself, with the guy who picked her up, and with the whole incident.

She was disappointed that she had upset her grandmother and dad by showing up at home in that condition. I listened to her tell her story and didn't speak until after she was finished. I found myself feeling angry and disappointed and was trying to keep a lid on those feelings. I said, "I'm really glad you survived the accident Chelsea, because it could have turned out a lot differently!" She heartily agreed. "But I'm also really disappointed that no one bothered to call me after it happened!"

She said, "Yeah, I'm really sorry about that. I was kind of busy."

I told her, "I know you were busy, but what about your dad calling me?" I was really trying not to get too emotional in front of her, but this was such a close call for her. It was really quite amazing that she had lived to tell about it! I was angry with her father for not calling me and frightened that we all could have lost her in this accident. I was stunned to say the least.

Over the next week or so, as Chelsea talked about what had happened and reflected on it, I gently reminded her that no one would ask a driver if he has a valid license or current insurance; we just blindly trust people who are driving. At first she thought her family was going to sue the driver for driving without a license. But then over time, she realized that the cost to hire an attorney to bring suit against him would cost as much or more than any money they might get out of the suit. She decided to just pay the deductible for her medical bills and be done with it.

While telling me this story, Chelsea admitted that she had been drinking alcohol with some old friends in her old home town quite regularly over the whole summer. Even though neither Chelsea nor the driver had been drinking before the accident, it made her think about her actions in the recent past. She told me she was sorry for drinking and for not being honest with me about it. She admitted that the whole "near death experience" with the car accident put a new perspective on her choices and what was really important in her life. She realized that drinking alcohol was not the solution to her problems and that hanging out with that particular crowd of people was not a good choice for her. She realized she needed to know the person behind the wheel of a car before she accepted a ride. She also talked about doing more things with her church so she would spend time with different—and potentially better—people.

Lessons Learned

The following week, after I had examined my reaction to her telling me about the car accident, I thought maybe I had over-reacted and sounded too much like a parent. I realized I gave her feedback when in fact, she had not asked for any. When we next got together, I told Chelsea that I had thought about my behavior the week before. I told her I thought I had gotten up on my soapbox and told her what she should or should not do. I did not want to assume she wanted my feedback. In the future, she would need to ask for feedback; I wasn't going to automatically offer it as if she wanted to hear from me.

Chelsea got a really worried look on her face and said, "But I REALLY DO want your feedback! That's why I tell you things—because you're a different kind of adult to talk to!"

I know that in order for her to tell me what's going on in her life, I need to have some level of neutrality and open-mindedness. Ranting and raving about the "should haves" or "could haves" doesn't change what happened. When Chelsea told me about the car accident I knew it was an important moment in our relationship. I said, "You know, ultimately, it doesn't matter what I say, your parents say, your teachers say, or anyone says. You have choices, and you will choose what you want to do. You make the choices, Chelsea. Nobody else can do it for you. You can listen to choices, and consider them, and choose one of them. But you will make the choices. I have no control over that. And I always hope that you will have a selection of choices from which to choose, and that you'll choose a good one for yourself." Whether we want to acknowledge it or not, teenagers can and will make adult decisions with less experience.

This incident put things in perspective for me. I was reminded that every day is a gift. My energy is best spent on enjoying my time with Chelsea and appreciating that she chooses to confide in me at all. I'm just glad she had an opportunity to live beyond the accident and learn some life lessons.

Final Thoughts

Every once in a while I find myself stressing about the fact that Chelsea has the ability to theoretically observe the various outcomes of her choices, but cannot fully realize the full implications on her future educational plans, career plans or life plans. I'm sure this is not a new way of thinking for adults who care about children. My parents probably had the same concerns. No matter how much I hope Chelsea doesn't encounter people with low integrity, illegal substances, alcohol or boys (or men!) with raging hormones, she will encounter all or some of them. All I can do to help her is to give her good information, educate her on how to make good decisions and help her believe in herself. I cannot be involved in every current or future decision she will make, but I can support her in being prepared to make good choices. When she makes her own choices and feels good about them, she can become more confident in making more choices as they present themselves. My challenge is to let her try out her skills as a decision maker and support her as she learns by doing.

Reflection: Resources for Tough Situations

Most of the drama or challenges I experienced with Chelsea occurred after we had separated from the original mentoring program and were on our own with her dad's blessing. I did a lot of "shooting from the hip" by trying to use some skills I learned through other situations, conferences I attended or books I read. Sometimes it worked and sometimes it didn't. You don't have to shoot from the hip—there's a better way. Besides staying in touch with your contact at the mentoring organization, I would highly recommend that you review the following resources available on my blog—www.YouthMentorIdeas.com.

1. **Take a look at the Crisis Resources for Girls and Women— National Hotlines**. These are resources for very serious situations, but knowing they exist—whether for your mentee, her family or someone else you care about—could be a huge help to someone in need.

2. **Flip through the Educational Resources for Girls and Women.** Find two resources that you think might come in handy with your mentee either now or when she gets older. IMPORTANT TIP: First review it yourself. Never give something to her that you haven't thoroughly looked over.

3. **The Working with Youth in Other Ways—A Starter List** offers additional ideas for working with young people outside of a one-on-one relationship. Think of the men and women you know who would be great working with kids. Send them a couple of website links and tell them, "You would be great at this—check it out!"

CHAPTER NINE

Activity Ideas

Mentoring is so important to success because
it can broaden your horizons and introduce you to a new world.
—Jackie Joyner-Kersee—

When I first got matched with Chelsea, I felt like I needed to use all my project management skills to fill up the time we spent together. I get nervous when silence falls between me and another person, and so I felt that the dreaded gaps in conversation could be avoided if I kept us busy. Couple the newness of our relationship with the mentoring rule "Don't ask probing questions—let her bring up things when she is ready," things were a bit challenging!

Sure, we zipped from one activity to another in the early days, but I found out that our most important and meaningful time together was our down time in the car or walking in a park. I realized that unscheduled time was special time. I didn't have to keep talking to fill up the space or rush from one thing to another to keep things interesting. Just being there and available to listen was valuable to Chelsea all by itself. She took advantage of our time as she saw fit—often seconds before I dropped her off at home at the end of the night! Sometimes it took all night for her to get up her courage to tell me something, but that was fine with me.

Scheduling Techniques That Work

As mentioned before, if you are mentoring a younger child (read: less than driving age) you will have to coordinate with her parents or guardian from a logistics perspective. Working out a system at the beginning of your relationship will help keep you sane. Communicating this schedule with your mentee to the other adults actively involved in her life is very important. To help make things run smoothly consider these techniques:

1. Coordinate calendars in a way that works for everybody involved.
2. Take turns with your mentee calling midweek to check in, touch base and verify the date and time of your next visit.
3. Make your time with your mentee a top priority.

Activity Ideas

Let me share a bit of mentoring wisdom in regards to time together: Activities don't need to be extra special, expensive or extraordinary to be fun for the both of you. "Run of the mill" errands or activities are perfectly fine because these involve time together and she gets you all to herself. She feels special, important and loved—whether she tells you or not. In the following pages I provide some ideas to work from and some approaches I've used that may be helpful to you.

Eating Together

When you pick her up, will you be eating a meal together? I always met with Chelsea after work on a Monday or Tuesday evening. I was always hungry and eating out was convenient. I chose to foot the bill for both of us as part of our time together. As a change of pace, you can both bring a bag lunch. (You might have to bring her a lunch depending on the supplies at her home or where you are picking her up.) If it's nice weather, go to a park and have a picnic. Have a picnic on your living room floor if the weather is not cooperating. Use coupons to get a discount on a meal or treat in the area. Buy an *Entertainment* book from your area; they work pretty well for almost anything and you get your money back in savings in no time.

Online coupons can be found on several websites: www.valpak.com, www.couponwinner.com, www.dealnews.com, www.extrabux.com or www.restaurant.com. Going directly to a restaurant website may also yield some coupons. Another approach to discounts is via www.groupon.com. Ask your friends to keep an eye out for coupons for the restaurants your mentee likes to go to or activities you would like to do with her.

What About Those Errands or Chores You Need to Do? Can She Be Your Helper?

Quality time shows up in very different ways. Chores and errands don't have to be put off to another day. (Of course it's not fair to look upon her as Cinderella either!) Working on these "necessary evils" in partnership can be helpful to you and fun for her. Why not put on some great music and have a little fun in the process? She can learn life skills that she can take home and into her adulthood, and her innocent questions and observations will certainly break up the work. Show her how to do the errands and chores as you go and give her more responsibility in the future.

A good rule of thumb for deciding which errand or chore to do during your time together is to always give her choices. That shows respect for her (rather than exerting your "adult authority") and gives her some control over how your time together will play out.

Here are some ideas for errands and chores that can be done together with your mentee:

- If you've been putting off grocery shopping for far too long, why not make it a field trip? Teach her how to go grocery shopping by showing her how to make a list, use coupons, purchase the items for a recipe, plan a party, use a calculator to keep track of cost, or write a check or use a credit card. Get her help to unload and put away groceries at your house. Idea: let her pick out one treat to store at your house for future visits.

- Pick up the dry cleaning. Get her help to carry the cleaned clothes and put them away when you get home.
- Visit the drugstore. While you're waiting for your prescription, have her go find other items for you that are located elsewhere in the store.
- Return the DVDs or library books and turn it into a trip to the library. Consider checking a DVD or book out for your night to-gether. If she doesn't have her own library card, help her sign up for one! Visit her own city library and ask for a tour from the librarian. If a tour is not available, show her around yourself and tell her how a library works. Help her find a book to check out and return the next time you get together.
- Buy supplies at the local home fix-it store or the office supplies store. Tell her what they're for and consider involving her in a home fix-it project during your time together.
- Buy gardening supplies and tools and plant flowers and vegetables.
- Rake the leaves and put the compost into bags at the curb. Play a radio for fun!
- Wash the car or vacuum the interior (play the car radio for fun!).
- Sort through that box of pictures in the closet and get her help to put them in photo albums.
- Fix a meal and clean up the kitchen.
- Do some laundry, fold the clothes together and put them away. (You might even do some of her laundry depending on her needs.)
- If her personal hygiene seems a bit compromised, perhaps a little at-home "spa night" is in order! Wash her hair, draw a bubble bath and make her feel special at your home.

A natural outgrowth of your "busy time" together is that the talks you will have will not all be superficial—you'll be surprised. She may find talking to you about a problem at school or home is easier when you're both doing something that is completely unrelated.

But don't forget—always make sure you have one-on-one girl time each time you get together. Your one-on-one time might be over a meal, while driving in your car (Chelsea's favorite talk location) or while helping her with her homework. Don't make your time all about errands and chores and running all over town. Always give her some of your undivided attention; this is an important part of any get-together. It sets a mentoring get-together apart from most other interactions she might have with adults.

Attend Her School Functions, Recitals, Sports or Recreation Events

Having family members see her perform is one level of excitement, but having her mentor attend is even better—at least that is what Chelsea tells me! I've brought my boyfriend to choir concerts, Pops concerts and solo singing competitions that Chelsea has been part of and we've always enjoyed them together. She and I can discuss them during our weekly time together because we shared the experience. You may not realize the significance you have in her life until she runs up to you after the show and gives you a big hug! She loves the attention and she is extremely pleased that you made the time to show her that she is special—especially in front of her school friends.

Schoolwork

Because your weekly time together will most likely take place after she gets home from school or on the weekend, you could get involved in helping her with homework. This isn't an absolute; I rarely helped Chelsea because she either got help at school or didn't have homework.

You can certainly offer help, but she needs to make the decision to accept your offer. She might be embarrassed to ask for help if her grades aren't good or she might be doing quite well and not need the assistance. Encourage her to show you her school projects or assignments that she is proud of so you are involved in that part of her life. Eventually she will feel more comfortable showing you those assignments where she didn't do as well because she trusts you and sees you as a source of support—no matter what kind of grade she gets. Again, connecting with her teachers and/or school counselors may be very helpful in understanding what is or is not going on at school for her and how you can help and support her.

Reading

Being resourceful is a useful quality for any person to have, especially as a mentor. As much as I tried to keep my "rescuing tendencies" under control, there were certain things that I thought were important and that needed my support as a mentor. When Chelsea was in middle school I was a little concerned that she didn't read for fun in her free time. I was not a reading expert and didn't know what her teachers were doing with her at school, so I decided to go online and do a Google search to find books that might be of interest to her. Somehow I got connected to a sort of "Ask the Librarian" feature in the New York Public Library. "What the heck?" I thought and sent the librarian an e-mail with my query. The librarian suggested *The Sisterhood of the Traveling Pants* books (there are now three) and a few others. In the next week or so I suggested to Chelsea that we go to her local library and track

Chelsea says...

When I was in sixth and seventh grade, I was at a second grade reading level. I didn't read well at all. I had really bad grammar, too. With Paula's support, I pretty much moved up all the way to a fifth grade reading level. I read a lot now. Even if I had more channels on my TV, I would still read. I like to read a lot more than any other form of entertainment, like movies or TV. Reading books to the kid I babysit helps my comprehension a lot, too. A lot of the books are the tongue-tied type books, and those are the best for your comprehension.

down the books. She checked out one of the "Sisterhood" books and ended up really liking it. WOO HOO! A few months later I bought her the second one in the series as a gift after she had her tonsils out. After that initial book, it seemed like she started reading more and more on her own and her confidence in her reading skills grew. She admits that it was a sort of turning point for her too.

Other Activity Ideas

Girl Power and Trusting Women

I liked to go to "girl power" movies with Chelsea because I wanted to expose her as often as possible to smart girls and women solving problems and using their strength to get through life. We always enjoyed Jodie Foster movies because that type of role is what Jodie plays very well. After a movie, I would often ask Chelsea, "What did you like?" and, "What didn't you like?" just to get a sense of what she thought about the movie. (I admit when she was younger and a PG-13 movie showed an unmarried couple in bed, I felt personally responsible for exposing Chelsea to "illicit activity" too early in life! But then, I was kidding myself, wasn't I!)

She is very much a romantic (her favorite movie is *The Notebook*) and she picks up on the deeper meaning of the story—if there is one. I believe any talks Chelsea and I have about positive themes relating to women support her as a female. I think when she can see herself in the characters and/or appreciate a quality or trait in a strong female character, a positive image stays with her in her own life experience. She has that character/movie/book/discussion to reflect upon when faced with her own challenges (home, school, work, relationships) and can make a similar choice or at least come from a stronger position as a result of that positive exposure. I like her to constantly see positive images of girls and women. I envision her gravitating towards people and environments that are supportive of her and her gender, versus putting up with people or environments that are not.

Other Activities

The list below and continuing on the next page represents some activity ideas. I've already talked about some of the ideas on this list but have included them again here so that you have a comprehensive checklist of activities. I'm sure you and your mentee will come up with many more ideas for things to do together. It's not a bad idea to write down the ideas you come up with together for future reference, whether it's with this mentee or with a future mentee.

Seventy-five Cool Activities for Mentors & Mentees!
Compliments of Paula & Chelsea

1. Play cards
2. Play games
3. Play catch/Frisbee
4. Plan and cook a meal
5. Do errands
6. Fly a kite
7. Watch and discuss a movie
8. Hang out and talk
9. Listen to and discuss an audio book
10. Do research on the Internet
11. Plan and plant a garden
12. Go bike riding or inline skating
13. Take a walk
14. Walk your dog
15. Eat at a restaurant
16. Play sports
17. Learn how to do laundry
18. Attend a sports event
19. Attend a concert
20. Learn a musical instrument
21. Learn to iron clothes
22. Write a story together
23. Go on a picnic
24. Get a library card and check out some books
25. Take photographs or videos
26. Use a computer software program together
27. Talk about your first job
28. Learn to read a map and use one while traveling
29. Give your mentee a tour of your workplace
30. Introduce your mentee to your family and family gatherings
31. Sell or buy something on eBay or Craigslist
32. Gather up items to donate and deliver to the Salvation Army or Goodwill
33. Buy a small amount of stock and watch the reports
34. Do woodworking
35. Go window shopping

Seventy-five Cool Activities for Mentors & Mentees!
Compliments of Paula & Chelsea (continued)

36. Plan a trip to a home remodeling store

37. Make a list and go grocery shopping

38. Wash the car

39. Play miniature golf

40. Spend time watching and talking about a TV show

41. Rent a DVD and make popcorn

42. Listen to each other's favorite music

43. Sing along with car radio songs

44. Take turns reading a book out loud

45. Go to the zoo and count the different animals

46. Go to the different museums in your town

47. Make cookies, Popsicles or cupcakes

48. Just listen and listen and listen!

49. Get a manicure or pedicure

50. Get a haircut

51. Do homework

52. Tell each other grandparent stories

53. Tell funny childhood stories

54. Create a super hero costume and take pictures of each other

55. Talk about your first love

56. Volunteer for a community project

57. Practice counting money and making change

58. Get an ice cream cone together

59. Invite your mentee to job-shadow you ("Bring Your Child to Work Day" is a fun day in the US)

60. Introduce your mentee to someone doing the work they fantasize about

61. Go swimming at the local pool

62. Show her how to make simple sewing repairs

63. Learn how to polish shoes

64. Create a résumé together

65. Fill out job applications together

66. Tour a college campus and learn how to enroll

67. Fill out financial aid applications

68. Fill out college applications

69. Talk about having a personal budget and how to make it work

70. Learn how to program an electronic device

71. Go to a book signing or author reading

72. Learn how to take care of pets

73. Learn a hobby together

74. Learn and practice bike repair

75. Write thank you notes for gifts

Preplanning Time Together

Sitting down once a month and talking about different things the two of you can do together is always a good place to start. I used to do it with Chelsea over dinner. I'd take lined paper and make three columns with the following headings:

Mentoring Preplanning Sheet		
Errands/Chores	**Sports/Recreation**	**Activities/Event**
Grocery shopping (5/5)	Rollerblading (5/19)	Library (5/5)
Dry cleaning (5/12)	Middle school football game (5/12)	Dollar movie night (5/24)
Hardware store (5/24)	Go for walk (4/29)	Hairstyling at my house (5/19)

Then we'd brainstorm on what kinds of things we could do (cheap is good!) and I'd have Chelsea fill them in on the sheet. We assigned a date to each item so we had a schedule for each get-together. It's always important to give her choices on what she wants to do and when it will be done if at all possible. Following through on the plans shows respect for her contributions too. If a change is required for any reason, make sure you explain why and give her a choice of alternate activities.

Most times preplanning worked pretty well and it gave me a bank of ideas to turn to when I was feeling brain-dead on the night we got together. The only challenge I found was whether an activity was available on the night we had scheduled it—not everything is! I did some basic online research to learn the operating hours for the local library, the zoo, the nature center, parks, etc. These are easy places to go to hang out, but you need to know if they're open.

As she got older, we sometimes sat in a local coffee shop and talked over a hot chocolate or even surfed the Internet using my laptop. Of course there's the inevitable "Let's go to the mall" request, but I always tried to steer her elsewhere whenever possible. If we hadn't preplanned our time, the mall is where we often headed.

Money: Keeping It in Perspective

Money may be in short supply in your life, or it may be quite available to spend as you choose. Whatever your situation with money, it is not meant to be the basis of your relationship with your mentee; it can be a part of your relationship if you choose. If you can afford to spend money on her, it's wonderful that you would like to make things or experiences available to her that may be in short supply at her home. That shows you are a generous and giving person. It also can set a precedent to your mentee that Mentor Outings = Expensive Activities.

When I got together with Chelsea each week, it was at my normal dinner hour and I was coming directly from work, so we normally went out to dinner together at the beginning of our visit. We went to our share of movies too, but it was normally because we hadn't preplanned our time together and I didn't want to go the mall yet again. The less we preplanned, the more money I seemed to spend.

Money Does Not "Buy" Connection

In a mentoring relationship the best way to truly connect is through the quality time, talks and support and trust that are built between two people sharing their lives together. An occasional, more expensive special event is fine. But complement that special event with many more simple, free or low-cost activities that emphasize your togetherness more than the event itself. Sometimes spending money is a "safer way" of telling her you care about her. Buying things for her will be well-appreciated in the moment but possibly forgotten in a few days or weeks. I would venture to say that looking in her eyes and telling her, "You're really a special girl—I'm glad I know you," or, "I look forward to our get-togethers every week!" or, "You have a funny sense of humor—you make me laugh so much!" are going to be much more memorable, meaningful and long-lasting gifts. In my mentoring opinion, money makes choices more available, but it doesn't buy meaningful, human connection.

Money Topics: Possible Ideas

Basic money management skills are not part of every family's experience. If your mentee does not have personal experience earning or spending money, or the adults in her family have not explained financial basics to her, this is an opportunity for you to share some useful information with her and turn money management into an activity! Here are some concepts to start with that will help put money in perspective.

Budgeting

1. When you take her to a special event, let her know how much money you have budgeted for her to spend on food, drinks or souvenirs while at the event. Help her figure out what she can buy and how much she'll have left after the purchase.
2. When you take her grocery shopping, let her know your grocery budget amount.
   - Let her keep track of the total cost on a calculator.
   - If you use coupons, discuss how you can save money by using them.
3. Discuss how budgeting money takes practice and discipline and what that looks like.

Saving Money

1. Talk about opening a savings account and why saving money is important.
   - Talk about what she would like to save money for in the future.
   - Talk about how she will earn money to save.

2. Talk about things you've saved money for and how you did it.
    - Talk about why an "I want it now!" mindset is not always the wisest way to live life.
    - Discuss how putting off buying things and going places sometimes makes more sense than doing it right away.
3. Talk about how you prioritize things and how that relates to money (e.g., a Christmas present for someone else is more important than a new top for me).
    - Get her involved in prioritizing purchases in terms of value and true importance.

ATM Cards

1. Discuss the pros and cons of ATM cards.
2. Discuss the importance of keeping receipts and keeping an account register.

Credit Cards

1. Discuss the pros and cons of owning a credit card.
2. Discuss living within your means versus living on borrowed money with an interest rate.

When You Have to Be Away: Staying Connected

Even though you may fully inform your mentee and her family that you will be out of town on business, vacation or dealing with family issues, she still misses your presence and might even feel a little bit abandoned (although she may not tell you right away). To stay connected, take a moment to send her a postcard or make a surprise phone call.

Chelsea has my cell phone number and she knows she can call me at any time. On occasion, I might pick up a small gift for her from my travel destination. But I truly believe, the more personal the contact, the better.

Final Thoughts

A lot of this is common sense and some of it involves making good decisions with the information you have available. Learn as you go. Ask questions of people who have good information. Always keep your mentee's best interests as a top priority. The next chapter shares some strategies that you as a powerful woman can employ to get more good men involved in mentoring. Help get the men back into mentoring!

Reflection: Activities

Make a starter list of inexpensive activities you might do with your mentee. You can use the table on the following page to write down your ideas. Ask for ideas from people with children. Look for activities in your local newspaper and park publications. Be sure to ask your mentee to add her own ideas too.

Activity Ideas		
	Activity	**Outdoor or Indoor?**
1		
2		
3		
4		
5		
6		
7		
8		
9		
10		

Getting Men Into Mentoring

Whether or not we realize it each of us has within us the ability to set
some kind of example for people. Knowing this, would you rather be
the one known for being the one who encouraged others, or the one who
inadvertently discouraged those around you?
—Josh Hinds—

One day a few years ago, Chelsea told me her dad was involved in a lunch time, school-based mentoring program through his employer. Chelsea told me the father of the little boy he was matched with had been killed in a motorcycle accident. Even with two sons and two daughters of his own, Chelsea's dad stepped up because he had been asked and because he knew the value of having a male role model. He recently told me his thoughts about mentoring:

"I think it's a great idea and a great philosophy. [Mentoring] really goes back to the community model of yester-year, where adults in the community shared in nurturing and raising children into mature adults. It takes a village! I have since been inspired to start mentoring inner city kids that have been placed by foster care into the suburbs; it's been a wonderful gift!"

If every man took a similar approach to prioritizing his life we would have all the male mentors that are needed.

Women: Choose Some Good Men

In the world of youth mentoring, the reality is there is a vast shortage of positive male role models to keep up with the boys that need them. Although female mentors are needed, there is a greater shortage of male mentors. This shortage of men is an across-the-board problem no matter the size of the mentoring program or the staff and budget it has available.

When I first mapped out the content for this book with Chelsea, I considered writing a book about youth mentoring "for all adults every-where." My early thoughts were something like, "EVERYBODY should be a mentor!" I still believe that, but I thought it made more sense to speak from a place of authority—the fact that I was a busy woman who was mentoring a girl. I thought credibility and firsthand experience should take precedence over trying to speak to every adult. My reality is, I am not a man! I don't think like a man and I don't understand what it's like to be a man, especially as it relates to youth mentoring.

I have spoken to many staff members from different mentoring organizations to enlist their support in inviting their mentors to pro-vide "Mentor Success Stories" for a companion book I was putting together, as well as to gather male mentor feedback for this chapter. All but one of the staff members I met with were women, which according to research is not unusual. Not only is there a shortage of male mentors, but there are fewer men working in the field of youth mentoring.

What Can We Do to Solve This Challenge?

Knowing that there is a shortage of men in youth mentoring, I didn't feel comfortable "ignoring" it in this book merely because I was the other gender. I decided to gather as much as I could on the topic—through feedback from male mentors and research on the topic—and provide some guidelines to my busy women readers so they could effectively recruit the men in their lives to be mentors.

Whether men want to admit it or not, women have a lot of clout when it comes to decision making! If you approach your father, brother, significant other or male coworker in a way that really speaks to him, you could help change the face of mentoring for boys too!

What the Male Mentors Say

Back in February, 2008 I met Kristina Marshall, President and CEO of Winning Futures! mentoring organization in Warren, Michigan and founder of the former Metro Detroit Mentor Collaboration (MDMC). She mentioned that the MDMC had conducted a survey with all of their male mentors to better understand men and mentoring and to learn how to effectively market to men and better address the shortage of male mentors. She graciously handed over the research to me for use in this book. I combined some of the anecdotal data with some other research I found from Mentor Michigan (www.michigan.gov/mentormichigan/) done by Kahle Research and the African American Male Leadership Institute. In fact, Mentor Michigan has an excellent "Men in Mentoring Toolkit" available on their website for free download.

I have provided some feedback from male mentors below specifically relating to the influence of women.

"I have been involved with coaching boys' Little League (as a young man and then again when my son got involved) and with Cub Scouts and Boy Scouts (again when my son got involved). Even though now I know that this is really an organized form of mentoring, at the time, I didn't see it that way. When my sister-in-law mentioned that she thought I would be great for a new mentoring program (Faces of the Future with Lori Fidler), I hemmed and hawed and said, 'Send me the info and I'll take a look.' What she did instead was call Lori and volunteer me for the program! Lori contacted me and asked for info and an interview and all the time I thought that I was just getting the general info until she came to interview me and it was then I realized I was trapped! The good news is that I have enjoyed the program (I'm on my second go around) and I still see one of my original mentees (his name is Shawn) regularly four years later. So the moral of the story…don't give us a choice!"

Jeff S.

Faces of the Future, Oak Park, MI

"I was divorced when I decided to mentor. I have been in a few relationships and every woman without exception thought very highly of what I was doing especially with my involvement on the board and other committee support I give. There have been a few articles in the paper with myself and my mentee and quite a number of women friends including my ex-wife called to say they saw it."

Gary P.

Mentor Connection, W. Bloomfield, MI

In the Metro Detroit Mentor Collaboration survey I mentioned previously, the (unidentified) male mentors gave some very interesting feedback about how women (including female mentoring organization staff) influenced them to become involved:

"She is very persuasive. Honestly, there was not a single event that prompted my action. The timing of the organization's founding and where I was in my life was just right. I know this does not give you a plan to replicate but that's just how it worked for me."

"She was very enthusiastic about the Guidance Center program."

"My daughter shared her experiences with the Guidance Center Mentor program that piqued my interest."

"I knew someone working with the program that I ultimately became a part of. She asked me if it would be something I was interested in. I decided that I was."

"She expressed her ongoing need for mentors and she thought I would be a good mentor."

"I initially inquired about a county mentoring program but was told by my wife, who has been active with Jewish Family Service, that JFS had a program as well."

"Reading the ad in the paper and talking with our daughter made me realize that it was time to get involved and the importance of volunteerism."

"My boss suggested that I should think about doing this after she saw a presentation by the Winning Futures staff asking for mentors."

"Yes, I was impressed with her programs to help students be successful."

"I know Kris from a class we had together and I saw her program firsthand. It was a program that I was impressed with and worked for me as well."

It's clear that women have persuasive powers; why not use our influence to make a huge difference in the lives of girls AND boys AND men?

Thirteen Ways to Turn Your Men Into Mentors

The list below summarizes some effective strategies for women to attract the men in their lives to mentoring boys.

1. **Make it personal:** Sit down with him, one on one, and invite him to become a mentor and tell him he would be a great one! Talk over a good meal. Put information and/or an application into his hands. Personal invitations rule!

2. **Support him in spreading his wonderfulness to another family who needs him via mentoring:** If he was wonderful to you and/ or your family now or in the past, isn't it a great gift to share him for a few hours a week with a boy who needs him? If he would otherwise be at home with you and/or family, your genuine support for him to mentor is critical.

3. **Use action words that might be more comfortable and familiar than "mentoring" ("mentoring" can be a scary word):** Use "advising," "supporting," "helping" or "leading" when describing a mentoring relationship.

4. **Men are often more comfortable "doing" than they are "feeling":** Talk about the positive outcomes and results of a mentoring relationship for both people. Talk about the activities, the places to go, the things to do and the topics that can be talked about with a boy. Avoid focusing on the "touchy-feely" stuff; that will come later when they bond together.

5. **Remind him that even if he didn't have a positive or available father figure of his own growing up, he can reflect upon the positive male role models he had in school, athletics, after-school activities, summer camp, work, the neighborhood, church and civic and professional organizations:** He has the capacity to personally become the positive male role model that another boy needs, based on his firsthand experience with positive role models.

6. **If he had a positive father figure in his life growing up, remind him how important that was and how his life would be very different without that influence:** As Gary P., a mentor with the Mentor Connection would say to a potential male mentor, "What if you never had a father in your life?" Just being a friend to a young boy can make all the difference in the world.

7. **Mentoring a boy does not have to be added to an already demanding schedule—it can be incorporated into his existing routine:** Remind him that quality time can be manifested in many different ways. In addition to an occasional game of catch, it could involve doing some yard work (while learning lawn maintenance skills and talking), running some errands together (car time talks, enjoying the ball game on the radio), or fixing a meal together at the man's home or sharing a meal and conversation at the local burger joint.

8. **Mentoring programs come in many "flavors"—structured or unstructured, community/school/church/special populations/ work/Internet-based:** There is a type of mentoring program for every man who has an interest. (The table in chapter 3 provides a comparison of mentoring programs.)

9. **He has the skills right now to be a mentor:** Remind him how he can teach a boy to do and enjoy things he already does at home and elsewhere (e.g., car repair, playing sports, lawn maintenance, playing a musical instrument, barbecuing, photography, woodworking, etc.). Help him envision sharing his activities with a boy.

10. **Mentoring organizations want him to be successful and enjoy the mentoring experience:** They provide orientations and training, and are available for any questions that come up. They need men to be mentors—now!

11. **"But what if I get accused of abuse or something?"** If a man is involved in a one-on-one, community-based program (unstructured, just the mentor and mentee spend time together) he will always be matched with a boy. All mentors—both men and women—must take part in several background checks before they are cleared to be a mentor. All mentors are in contact with

a program staff person who not only knows the young person but his family too. Any concern that may arise—big or small— should be shared with program staff immediately so it can be discussed and handled appropriately.

12. **If he doesn't tend to listen to you about the importance of community service and/or making time to volunteer, recruit another male mentor/coach that he respects to approach him:** Sometimes other men can do "guy-speak" better.

13. **Watch a movie about mentoring:** Some great male-mentoring movies to foster that "mentoring state of mind" include: *The Karate Kid, Finding Forrester, Antoine Fisher, Coach Carter, Remember the Titans, Good Will Hunting, Dead Poet's Society, In Search of Bobby Fisher* and *Gran Torino*. (Make sure the mentoring application is sitting next to the remote control!)

Final Thoughts

In March of 2008, Chelsea and I were asked to speak at the mentor support meeting for the program where we got our start back in 2001, Mentors Plus of Oakland County, Michigan. We were the featured speakers since we were "alumni" and budding authors. I asked the group in attendance to participate in my online surveys for both "Mentor Success Stories" and "Male Mentor feedback." A response from one of the two men in attendance is below.

"I have been the Chair of the Birmingham Mentors Plus program for over eleven years now. The biggest challenge has been to get other men to volunteer. I, in general, have been the only male mentor for any sustained period during my eleven years. Although I talk it up as much as possible, I think that people are generally too absorbed in their own lives to consider giving time to kids they don't know or with whom there is no personal connection. I guess the most important message to "seal the deal" is that volunteering can be incorporated into your own routine and it really doesn't have to take that much time. The mentor also gets a great deal back from the relationship. Finally, I think it's important to give back to the community with no expectation of personal gain/benefit. 'To those whom much is given, much is expected'."

David W.
Mentors Plus, Birmingham, MI

David is one of the "good guys" who continues to stay involved in mentoring no matter what. As I recall, he has mentored about six different boys in the eleven years he has been a mentor. That is dedication! Although David told me his wife is always supportive of his volunteer activities, he was originally invited to get involved in mentoring through the invitation of a fellow (male) Optimist Club member. Having been a former Eagle Scout, he understood the value of positive role models and wanted to reach out to a boy who needed one through a mentoring program.

Your supportive words and schedule adjustments can communicate to the man in your life—in a powerful way—that you believe he has valuable qualities and skills to share, he is a wonderful role model and that you are proud to share him with a boy who needs him. Who is waiting to hear this message from you? Your father? Your significant other? Your brother? Your nephew? Your grandson? A coworker? A church member? A neighbor? You have power and influence as a woman; spread it around and start changing the lives of boys and the men that you know and love. Use your "woman power" and help get the men back into mentoring!

Reflection: All the Good Men

Make a list of all the good men that you know who you believe would make great mentors to boys. Contact them and tell them you have started mentoring a girl. Explain that there is always a shortage of good male mentors and that you thought he would make a great match.

Good Male Mentor Prospects	
1	
2	
3	
4	
5	
6	
7	
8	
9	
10	

Poetry

By: Chelsea McKinney

My hand and heart become one
All emotions pour out,
As lead scrapes the page,
The earth around me is still,

Not a care in the world
As my poem comes to mind
My mind is numb,
Yet my heart is set,

Seeing a puffy cloud in the sky
Or a crisp autumn leaf,
My hand beats a rhythm,
Words come in play,

Poetry is like a smile
A brisk winter morning,
Sky bright, the air stings my face,

When they come out on paper
After I read
I was in a poetic trance

Epilogue

When work, commitment, and pleasure all become one and you reach that
deep well where passion lives, nothing is impossible.
—Nancy Coey—

Who would've thought that ten plus years later Chelsea and I would still have a similar weekly routine? Certainly not me! (I can plan vacations well ahead of time, but NOT relationships.) Now, instead of hearing about the world of a cute, insecure, awkward eleven-year-old girl who is desperate for a "best friend" and still reeling from her parents' divorce, I hear about the world of a beautiful, thoughtful twenty-one-year-old young woman.

As a young adult, Chelsea has learned much about herself and why people behave the way they do under some very challenging circumstances. She has some good friends, is making better choices and is passionately committed to "being the change" for children with special needs by becoming an Occupational Therapist. Chelsea has done well in spite of many obstacles and now has a focus in her life.

Quite frankly I cannot take sole credit for the young woman she has turned out to be or the accomplishments she has experienced. Chelsea took those actions herself, which is exactly the way it should be. But what I can claim is that I made the commitment to spend weekly time with a child for a year, back in the summer of 2000. I was willing to jump in and figure things out because I believed that making a difference in the life of a child was an important thing to do, whether it was comfortable for me or not. I am proud of myself for doing so and even prouder of Chelsea for "hanging in there" through a challenging childhood. I'm truly pleased to have been part of her life and for the opportunity to know her family and some of her friends.

Since I have been interacting with Chelsea's family for so many years, I decided to ask them a number of questions about what they thought of mentoring and how it has affected Chelsea. When I first met Chelsea, George was a single parent with four children. Joshua was about nine years old and Jacob was six. (Samantha is Chelsea's older sister, but was not available for comment.)

How do you think having a mentor has affected Chelsea?

"Chelsea has always felt that she had one unbiased adult in her life that she could go to especially when life had become too complicated or distracting for the adults in her life to really be there for her. It was especially helpful when she was trying to navigate young adulthood and too hurt or ashamed to ask for help getting herself back on track." (George)

"Socially, Chelsea has always been outgoing. However, after her experience being mentored, I noticed that she was more able to apply this social skill in real life." (Josh)

"I think it has built her to be a better person all around." (Jacob)

Did you have an opportunity to meet or get to know Paula? What was your impression of Paula as Chelsea's mentor?

"Throughout the years, Paula has been a major participant in Chelsea's life, and has attended every school play, graduation, church function, etc. that I can remember. I cannot recall the first time that I met Paula, but what I can bear witness to is her great devotion to Chelsea and the whole family." (Joshua)

"Yes, she is a very kind caring person and is also fun to be around with her charismatic qualities."(Jacob)

What do you think of the whole idea of an adult volunteer serving as a mentor/positive adult role model to a girl (or boy) who needs one? Why?

"I am personally a big advocate of it. When a parent figure is unavailable or insufficient, a solid role model for the child or even adolescent can be key to behavior, socialization, and productivity in school and in the future of the child." (Joshua)

"Personally I think it is a great idea. I had one at school and it was nice to have somebody who was able to relate and who enjoyed talking to me weekly." (Jacob)

Both Chelsea and I hope you can grow a wonderful mentoring relationship like ours. Just say yes to mentoring!

-Paula C. Dirkes & Chelsea M. McKinney

Here is a test to find whether your mission on earth is finished: if you're alive, it isn't.

—Richard Bach—

Please Join Me!

I would like to invite you to visit www.YouthMentorIdeas.com where I share my thoughts about mentoring, its impact on my life and the many lessons I have learned (and continue to learn) as a mentor.

I would like to hear about your experiences as a mentor as well. Share your stories and insights about mentoring on Facebook at www.facebook.com/MentorMeBook.

Please feel free to contact me at: info@youthmentorideas.com

Paula C. Dirkes
October, 2011

References

Alliance for Excellent Education (2006). *Healthier and wealthier: Decreasing healthcare costs by increasing educational attainment.* Issue Brief, Washington, DC: Alliance for Excellent Education.

Dubois, D. L., & Karcher, M. J. (Eds.) (2005). *Handbook of youth mentoring.* Thousand Oaks, CA: Sage Publications, Inc.

Editorial Projects in Education & The EPE Research Center (2010). Diplomas count [Special Issue]. *Education Week, 29*(34).

Emery, R. E. (1988). *Marriage, divorce and children's adjustment.* Thousand Oaks, CA: Sage Publications, Inc.

Garringer, M. (2004). Putting the "men" back into mentoring. *The National Mentoring Center Bulletin, 2.* Retrieved September 17, 2008, from http://www.nwrel.org/mentoring/pdf/v2n2.pdf.

Garringer, M., & Jucovy, L. (n.d.). *Building relationships: A guide for new mentors.* Retrieved September 18, 2008, from http://www.nwrel.org/mentoring/topic_pubs.php#6.

Jekielele, S.M., Moore, K.A., Hair, E. C., & Scarupa, H.J. (2002). *Child Trends Brief Mentoring: A promising strategy for youth development.* Retrieved June 10, 2011, from http://www.childtrends.org/Files/MentoringBrief2002.pdf.

Jucovy, Linda. (2000). *The ABCs of school-based mentoring.* Retrieved August 29, 2008, from http://www.ppv.org/ppv/publications/assets/32_publication.pdf.

Kahle Research Solutions Inc. & Mentor Michigan (2006). *Men and mentoring: A systematic review of available information.* Unpublished research paper.

Kurdek, L.A., & Fine, M.A. (1993). The relation between family structure and young adolescents appraisals of family climate and parenting behavior. *Journal of Family Issues, 14 ,* 279-290.

Marshall, K. (2007). *Metro Detroit Mentor Collaboration male mentor survey.* Unpublished raw data.

National Judicial College. (1997). *Crime, Courts and Christ: Helping the offender grow from law breaking to law abiding to a life with Jesus.* [Brochure]. Leenhouts, KJ: Author.

The American Heritage college dictionary (4th ed.). (2002). Boston, MA: Houghton Mifflin Harcourt Company.

Probst, K. (2006). *Mentoring for meaningful results: Asset-building tips, tools, and activities for youth and adults.* Minneapolis, MN: Search Institute.

Rouse, C. (2005). Labor market consequences of an inadequate education. *Symposium on the social costs of inadequate education,* New York, NY.

Tierney, J.P., Grossman, J.B., & Resch, N.L. (1995). *Making a difference: An impact study of Big Brothers/Big Sisters.* Philadelphia: Public/Private Ventures.

UNICEF Innocenti Research Centre. (2001, July). *A league table of teenage births in rich nations* (Innocenti Report Card No. 3). Florence, Italy: Author

U.S. Bureau of the Census. (2006). *Statistical abstract of the United States* (122nd edition). Washington, DC: US Government Printing Office.

Weinberger, S. G. (2005). Developing a mentoring program. In D.L. Dubois, & M.J. Karcher (Eds.), *Handbook of youth mentoring* (p. 220). Thousand Oaks, CA: Sage Publications, Inc.

Zimmerman, M. A., Bingenheimer, J. B., & Behrendt, D. E. (2005). Natural mentoring relationships. In D.L. Dubois, & M.J. Karcher (Eds.), *Handbook of youth mentoring* (pp. 143-144). Thousand Oaks, CA: Sage Publications, Inc.

Order Information

To order additional copies of this book or other related products, please choose one of the following methods:

☎   Telephone: 1-877-407-9586

@   E-mail: orders@FutureGenerationsPublishing.com

🛍   Online orders: www.MentorMeBook.com

Future Generations Publishing

Ask us about other products or services offered by
Paula Dirkes or
Future Generations Publishing:

◦ Books/Reports   ◦ Speaking/Seminars   ◦ Consulting

Please contact our office toll free at 1-877-407-9586 and leave a detailed message. We will respond within one business day.

Thank you for your interest!

Author Bios

Paula Dirkes earned her BS in secondary education from Michigan State University and her MA in Human Performance Improvement from the University of Michigan. She has taught and coached junior high school students in Lansing, Michigan and worked with infants through college students as the Youth & Aquatic Director at the Lansing Central YMCA. Since 2001 she has been an active community-based mentor to Chelsea McKinney, a faith-based mentor for twelve- to eighteen-year-old boys and girls at Renaissance Unity church in Warren, Michigan, a school-based mentor/coach in the Teen Leadership program at Hazel Park High School, a repeat adult volunteer at over twenty-five Challenge Day programs at numerous secondary schools in metro Detroit as well as a one-on-one tutor for grade school children at Timbuktu Academy of Science and Technology in east Detroit.

Paula is an active speaker for mentoring organizations, professional organizations, churches and schools and a youth mentoring advocate. She published two digital books in 2008: *MENTORrific Women! Taking a Girl Under Your Wing* and *MENTORrific Success Stories: Inspiring Stories from Youth Mentors & Mentees*. She lives in Berkley, Michigan.

Chelsea McKinney is a high school graduate and is currently pursuing post-secondary education. She has a true appreciation of how mentoring has changed her life, which motivated her to contribute to this book in the hopes that more women will get involved in mentoring and change the lives of other children. She definitely plans to be a mentor herself one day. Chelsea loves working with children and plans to pursue an Occupational Therapy degree. She enjoys spending time with her family when she is not in school. She lives in Howell, Michigan.

CPSIA information can be obtained
at www.ICGtesting.com
Printed in the USA
FFOW01n1133120216
21330FF